ECKERMANN'S CONVERSATIONS WITH GOETHE

ECKERMANN'S CONVERSATIONS WITH GOETHE

JOHANN WOLFGANG VON GOETHE,
JOHN OXENFORD

ISBN: 978-93-89560-58-9

Published: 1914

LECTOR HOUSE LLP
E-MAIL: lectorpublishing@gmail.com

ECKERMANN'S CONVERSATIONS WITH GOETHE

(EXTRACTS FROM THE AUTHOR'S PREFACE.)

BY

JOHANN WOLFGANG VON GOETHE

TRANSLATED BY
JOHN OXENFORD

1914

LIST OF ILLUSTRATIONS

Page

I. GOETHE'S STUDY 2

II. THE GARDEN AT GOETHE'S CITY HOUSE WEIMAR
(AFTER A WATER COLOR BY PETER WOLTZE) 6

III. SCHILLER'S GARDEN HOUSE AT JENA (DRAWING
BY GOETHE). 50

IV. THE MOAT AT JENA (DRAWING BY GOETHE) 52

V. VIEW INTO THE SAALE VALLEY NEAR JENA (DRAW-
ING BY GOETHE) 54

ECKERMANN'S CONVERSATIONS WITH GOETHE

This collection of Conversations with Goethe took its rise chiefly from an impulse, natural to my mind, to appropriate to myself by writing any part of my experience which strikes me as valuable or remarkable.

Moreover, I felt constantly the need of instruction, not only when I first met with that extraordinary man, but also after I had lived with him for years; and I loved to seize on the import of his words, and to note it down, that I might possess them for the rest of my life.

When I think how rich and full were the communications by which he made me so happy for a period of nine years, and now observe how small a part I have retained in writing, I seem to myself like a child who, endeavoring to catch the refreshing spring shower with open hands, finds that the greater part of it runs through his fingers.

* * * * *

I think that these conversations not only contain many valuable explanations and instructions on science, art, and practical life, but that these sketches of Goethe, taken directly from life, will be especially serviceable in completing the portrait which each reader may have formed of Goethe from his manifold works.

Still, I am far from imagining that the whole internal Goethe is here adequately portrayed. We may, with propriety, compare this extraordinary mind and man to a many-sided diamond, which in each direction shines with a different hue. And as, under different circumstances and with different persons, he became another being, so I, too, can only say, in a very modest sense, this is *my* Goethe.

* * * * *

GOETHE'S STUDY

My relation to him was peculiar, and of a very intimate kind: it was that of the scholar to the master; of the son to the father; of the poor in culture to the rich in culture. He drew me into his own circle, and let me participate in the mental and bodily enjoyments of a higher state of existence. Sometimes I saw him but once a week, when I visited him in the evening; sometimes every day, when I had the happiness to dine with him either alone or in company. His conversation was as varied as his works. He was always the same, and always different. Now he was occupied by some great idea, and his words flowed forth rich and inexhaustible; they were often like a garden in spring where all is in blossom, and where one is so dazzled by the general brilliancy that one does not think of gathering a nosegay. At other times, on the contrary, he was taciturn and laconic, as if a cloud pressed upon his soul; nay, there were days when it seemed as if he were filled with icy coldness, and a keen wind was sweeping over plains of frost and snow. When one saw him again he was again like a smiling summer's day, when all the warblers of the wood joyously greet us from hedges and bushes, when the cuckoo's voice resounds through the blue sky, and the brook ripples through flowery meadows. Then it was a pleasure to hear him; his presence then had a beneficial influence, and the heart expanded at his words.

Winter and summer, age and youth, seemed with him to be engaged in a perpetual strife and change; nevertheless, it was admirable in him, when from seventy to eighty years old, that youth always recovered the ascendancy; those autumnal and wintry days I have indicated were only rare exceptions.

His self-control was great—nay, it formed a prominent peculiarity in his character. It was akin to that lofty deliberation (*Besonnenheit*) through which he always succeeded in mastering his material, and giving his single works that artistical finish which we admire in them. Through the same quality he was often concise and circumspect, not only in many of his writings, but also in his oral expressions.

When, however, in happy moments, a more powerful demon[1] was active within him, and that self-control abandoned him, his discourse rolled forth with youthful impetuosity, like a mountain cataract. In such moments he expressed what was best and greatest in his abundant nature, and such moments are to be understood when his earlier friends say of him, that his spoken words were better than those which he wrote and printed. Thus Marmontel said of Diderot, that whoever knew him from his writings only knew him but half; but that as soon as he became animated in actual conversation he was incomparable, and irresistibly carried his hearers along.

* * * * *

1823

_Weimar, June 10.[2]—I arrived here a few days ago, but did not see Goethe till today. He received me with great cordiality; and the impression he made on me was such, that I consider this day as one of the happiest in my life.

Yesterday, when I called to inquire, he fixed today at twelve o'clock as the

---

[1] It is almost needless to observe that the word "demon" is her reference to its Greek origin, and implies nothing evil.—*Trans.*

[2] This is the first day in Eckermann's first book, and the first time in which he speaks in this book, as distinguished from Soret.—*Trans.*

time when he would be glad to see me. I went at the appointed time, and found a servant waiting for me, preparing to conduct me to him.

The interior of the house made a very pleasant impression upon me; without being showy, everything was extremely simple and noble; even the casts from antique statues, placed upon the stairs, indicated Goethe's especial partiality for plastic art, and for Grecian antiquity. I saw several ladies moving busily about in the lower part of the house, and one of Ottilie's beautiful boys, who came familiarly up to me, and looked fixedly in my face.

After I had cast a glance around, I ascended the stairs, with the very talkative servant, to the first floor.

He opened a room, on the threshold of which the motto *Salve* was stepped over as a good omen of a friendly welcome. He led me through this apartment and opened another, somewhat more spacious, where he requested me to wait, while he went to announce me to his master. The air here was most cool and refreshing; on the floor was spread a carpet; the room was furnished with a crimson sofa and chairs, which gave a cheerful aspect; on one side stood a piano; and the walls were adorned with many pictures and drawings, of various sorts and sizes.

Through an open door opposite, one looked into a farther room, also hung with pictures, through which the servant had gone to announce me.

It was not long before Goethe came in, dressed in a blue frock-coat, and with shoes. What a sublime form! The impression upon me was surprising. But he soon dispelled all uneasiness by the kindest words. We sat down on the sofa. I felt in a happy perplexity, through his look and his presence, and could say little or nothing.

He began by speaking of my manuscript. "I have just come from *you*," said he; "I have been reading your writing all the morning; it needs no recommendation—it recommends itself." He praised the clearness of the style, the flow of the thought, and the peculiarity that all rested on a solid basis and had been thoroughly considered. "I will soon forward it," said he; "today I shall write to Cotta by post, and send him the parcel tomorrow." I thanked him with words and looks.

We then talked of my proposed excursion. I told him that my design was to go into the Rhineland, where I intended to stay at a suitable place, and write something new. First, however, I would go to Jena, and there await Herr von Cotta's answer.

Goethe asked whether I had acquaintance in Jena. I replied that I hoped to come in contact with Herr von Knebel; on which he promised me a letter which would insure me a more favorable reception. "And, indeed," said he, "while you are in Jena, we shall be near neighbors, and can see or write to one another as often as we please." We sat a long while together, in a tranquil, affectionate mood. I was close to him; I forgot to speak for looking at him—I could not look enough. His face is so powerful and brown! full of wrinkles, and each wrinkle full of expression! And everywhere there is such nobleness and firmness, such repose and greatness! He spoke in a slow, composed manner, such as you would expect from an aged monarch. You perceive by his air that he reposes upon himself, and is elevated far above both praise and blame. I was extremely happy near him; I felt becalmed like one who, after many toils and tedious expectations, finally sees his dearest wishes gratified.

Thursday, September 18.—"The world is so great and rich, and life so full of variety, that you can never want occasions for poems. But they must all be occasional[3] poems; that is to say, reality must give both impulse and material for their production. A particular case becomes universal and poetic by the very circumstance that it is treated by a poet. All my poems are occasional poems, suggested by real life, and having therein a firm foundation. I attach no value to poems snatched out of the air.

"Let no one say that reality wants poetical interest; for in this the poet proves his vocation, that he has the art to win from a common subject an interesting side. Reality must give the motive, the points to be expressed, the kernel, as I may say; but to work out of it a beautiful, animated whole, belongs to the poet. You know Fürnstein, called the Poet of Nature; he has written the prettiest poem possible, on the cultivation of hops.

"I have now proposed to him to make songs for the different crafts of working-men, particularly a weaver's song, and I am sure he will do it well, for he has lived among such people from his youth; he understands the subject thoroughly, and is therefore master of his material. That is exactly the advantage of small works; you need only choose those subjects of which you are master. With a great poem, this cannot be: no part can be evaded; all which belongs to the animation of the whole, and is interwoven into the plan, must be represented with precision. In youth, however, the knowledge of things is only one-sided. A great work requires many-sidedness, and on that rock the young author splits."

---

[3] The word "Gelegenheitsgedicht" (occasional poem) properly applies to poems written for special occasions, such as birthdays, weddings, etc., but Goethe here extends the meaning, as he himself explains. As the English word "occasional" often implies no more than "occurrence now and then," the phrase "occasional poem" is not very happy, and is only used for want of a better. The reader must conceive the word in the limited sense, produced on some special event.—*Trans.*

THE GARDEN AT GOETHE'S CITY HOUSE WEIMAR (AFTER A WATER COLOR BY PETER WOLTZE)

I told Goethe that I had contemplated writing a great poem upon the seasons, in which I might interweave the employments and amusements of all classes. "Here is the very case in point," replied Goethe; "you may succeed in many parts, but fail in others which refer to what you have not duly investigated. Perhaps you would do the fisherman well, and the huntsman ill; and if you fail anywhere, the whole is a failure, however good single parts may be, and you have not produced a perfect work. Give separately the single parts to which you are equal, and you make sure of something good.

"I especially warn you against great inventions of your own; for then you would try to give a view of things, and for that purpose youth is seldom ripe. Further, character and views detach themselves as sides from the poet's mind, and deprive him of the fulness requisite for future productions. And, finally, how much time is lost in invention, internal arrangement, and combination, for which nobody thanks us, even supposing our work is happily accomplished.

"With a *given* material, on the other hand, all goes easier and better. Facts and characters being provided, the poet has only the task of animating the whole. He preserves his own fulness, for he needs to part with but little of himself, and there is much less loss of time and power, since he has only the trouble of execution. Indeed, I would advise the choice of subjects which have been worked before. How many Iphigenias have been written! yet they are all different, for each writer considers and arranges the subject differently; namely, after his own fashion.

"But, for the present, you had better lay aside all great undertakings. You have striven long enough; it is time that you should enter into the cheerful period of life, and for the attainment of this, the working out of small subjects is the best expedient."

Sunday, October 19.—Today, I dined for the first time with Goethe. No one was present except Frau von Goethe, Fräulein Ulrica, and little Walter, and thus we were all very comfortable. Goethe appeared now solely as father of a family, helping to all the dishes, carving the roast fowls with great dexterity, and not forgetting between whiles to fill the glasses. We had much lively chat about the theatre, young English people, and other topics of the day; Fräulein Ulrica was especially lively and entertaining. Goethe was generally silent, coming out only now and then with some pertinent remark. From time to time he glanced at the newspaper, now and then reading us some passages, especially about the progress of the Greeks.

They then talked about the necessity of my learning English, and Goethe earnestly advised me to do so, particularly on account of Lord Byron; saying, that a character of such eminence had never existed before, and probably would never come again. They discussed the merits of the different teachers here, but found none with a thoroughly good pronunciation; on which account they deemed it better to go to some young Englishman.

After dinner, Goethe showed me some experiments relating to his theory of colors. The subject was, however, new to me; I neither understood the phenomena, nor what he said about them. Nevertheless, I hoped that the future would afford me leisure and opportunity to initiate myself a little into this science.

* * * * *

Thursday, November 13.—Some days ago, as I was walking one fine afternoon towards Erfurt, I was joined by an elderly man, whom I supposed, from his appearance, to be an opulent citizen. We had not talked together long, before the conversation turned upon Goethe. I asked him whether he knew Goethe. "Know him?" said he, with some delight; "I was his valet almost twenty years!" He then launched into the praises of his former master. I begged to hear something of

Goethe's youth, and he gladly consented to gratify me.

"When I first lived with him," said he, "he might have been about twenty-seven years old; he was thin, nimble, and elegant in his person. I could easily have carried him in my arms."

I asked whether Goethe, in that early part of his life here, had not been very gay. "Certainly," replied he; "he was always gay with the gay, but never when they passed a certain limit; in that case he usually became grave. Always working and seeking; his mind always bent on art and science; that was generally the way with my master. The duke often visited him in the evening, and then they often talked on learned topics till late at night, so that I got extremely tired, and wondered when the duke would go. Even then he was interested in natural science.

"One time he rang in the middle of the night, and when I entered his room I found he had rolled his iron bed to the window, and was lying there, looking out upon the heavens. 'Have you seen nothing in the sky?' asked he; and when I answered in the negative, he bade me run to the guard-house, and ask the man on duty if he had seen nothing. I went there; the guard said he had seen nothing, and I returned with this answer to my master, who was still in the same position, lying in his bed, and gazing upon the sky. 'Listen,' said he to me; 'this is an important moment; there is now an earthquake, or one is just going to take place;' then he made me sit down on the bed, and showed me by what signs he knew this."

I asked the good old man "what sort of weather it was." "It was very cloudy," he replied; "no air stirring; very still and sultry."

I asked if he at once believed there was an earthquake on Goethe's word.

"Yes," said he, "I believed it, for things always happened as he said they would. Next day he related his observations at court, when a lady whispered to her neighbor, 'Only listen, Goethe is dreaming.' But the duke, and all the men present, believed Goethe, and the correctness of his observations was soon confirmed; for, in a few weeks, the news came that a part of Messina, on that night, had been destroyed by an earthquake."

Friday, November 14.—Towards evening Goethe sent me an invitation to call upon him. Humboldt, he said, was at court, and therefore I should be all the more welcome. I found him, as I did some days ago, sitting in his armchair; he gave me a friendly shake of the hand, and spoke to me with heavenly mildness. The chancellor soon joined us. We sat near Goethe, and carried on a light conversation, that he might only have to listen. The physician, Counsellor Rehbein, soon came also. To use his own expression, he found Goethe's pulse quite lively and easy. At this we were highly pleased, and joked with Goethe on the subject. "If I could only get rid of the pain in my left side!" he said. Rehbein prescribed a plaster there; we talked on the good effect of such a remedy, and Goethe consented to it. Rehbein turned the conversation to Marienbad, and this appeared to awaken pleasant reminiscences in Goethe. Arrangements were made to go there again, it was said that the great duke would join the party, and these prospects put Goethe in the most cheerful mood. They also talked about Madame Szymanowska, and mentioned the time when she was here, and all the men were solicitous for her favor.

When Rehbein was gone, the chancellor read the Indian poems, and Goethe, in the meanwhile, talked to me about the Marienbad Elegy.

At eight o'clock, the chancellor went, and I was going, too, but Goethe bade me stop a little, and I sat down. The conversation turned on the stage, and the fact that *Wallenstein* was to be done tomorrow. This gave occasion to talk about Schiller.

"I have," said I, "a peculiar feeling towards Schiller. Some scenes of his great dramas I read with genuine love and admiration; but presently I meet with something which violates the truth of nature, and I can go no further. I feel this even in reading *Wallenstein*. I cannot but think that Schiller's turn for philosophy injured his poetry, because this led him to consider the idea far higher than all nature; indeed, thus to annihilate nature. What he could conceive must happen, whether it were in conformity with nature or not."

"It was sad," said Goethe, "to see how so highly gifted a man tormented himself with philosophical disquisitions which could in no way profit him. Humboldt has shown me letters which Schiller wrote to him in those unblest days of speculation. There we see how he plagued himself with the design of perfectly separating sentimental from *naive* poetry. For the former he could find no proper soil, and this brought him into unspeakable perplexity."

"As if," continued he, smiling, "sentimental poetry could exist at all without the *naive* ground in which, as it were, it has its root."

"It was not Schiller's plan," continued Goethe, "to go to work with a certain unconsciousness, and as it were instinctively; he was forced, on the contrary, to reflect on all he did. Hence it was that he never could leave off talking about his poetical projects, and thus he discussed with me all his late pieces, scene after scene.

"On the other hand, it was contrary to my nature to talk over my poetic plans with anybody—even with Schiller. I carried everything about with me in silence, and usually nothing was known to any one till the whole was completed. When I showed Schiller my *Hermann and Dorothea* finished, he was astonished, for I had said not a syllable to him of any such plan.

"But I am curious to hear what you will say of *Wallenstein* tomorrow. You will see noble forms, and the piece will make an impression on you such as you probably do not dream of."

Saturday, November 15.—In the evening I was in the theatre, where I for the first time saw *Wallenstein*. Goethe had not said too much; the impression was great, and stirred my inmost soul. The actors, who had almost all belonged to the time when they were under the personal influence of Schiller and Goethe, gave an ensemble of significant personages, such as on a mere reading were not presented to my imagination with all their individuality. On this account the piece had an extraordinary effect upon me, and I could not get it out of my head the whole night.

Sunday, November 16.—In the evening at Goethe's; he was still sitting in his elbow-chair, and seemed rather weak. His first question was about *Wallenstein*. I gave him an account of the impression the piece had made upon me as represented on the stage, and he heard me with visible satisfaction.

M. Soret came in, led in by Frau von Goethe, and remained about an hour. He brought from the duke some gold medals, and by showing and talking about these seemed to entertain Goethe very pleasantly.

Frau von Goethe and M. Soret went to court, and I was left alone with Goethe.

Remembering his promise to show me again his Marienbad Elegy at a fitting opportunity, Goethe arose, put a light on the table, and gave me the poem. I was delighted to have it once more before me. He quietly seated himself again, and left me to an undisturbed perusal of the piece.

After I had been reading a while, I turned to say something to him, but he seemed to be asleep. I therefore used the favorable moment, and read the poem again and again with a rare delight. The most youthful glow of love, tempered by the moral elevation of the mind, seemed to me its pervading characteristic. Then I thought that the feelings were more strongly expressed than we are accustomed to find in Goethe's other poems, and imputed this to the influence of Byron—which Goethe did not deny.

"You see the product of a highly impassioned mood," said he. "While I was in it I would not for the world have been without it, and now I would not for any consideration fall into it again.

"I wrote that poem immediately after leaving Marienbad, while the feeling of all I had experienced there was fresh. At eight in the morning, when we stopped at the first stage, I wrote down the first strophe; and thus I went on composing in the carriage, and writing down at every stage what I had just composed in my head, so that by the evening the whole was on paper. Thence it has a certain directness, and is, as I may say, poured out at once, which may be an advantage to it as a whole."

"It is," said I, "quite peculiar in its kind, and recalls no other poem of yours."

"That," said he, I "may be, because I staked upon the present moment as a man stakes a considerable sum upon a card, and sought to enhance its value as much as I could without exaggeration."

These words struck me as very important, inasmuch as they threw a light on Goethe's method so as to explain that many-sidedness which has excited so much admiration.

1824

Friday, January 2.—Dined at Goethe's, and enjoyed some cheerful conversation. Mention was made of a young beauty belonging to the Weimar society, when one of the guests remarked that he was on the point of falling in love with her, although her understanding could not exactly be called brilliant.

"Pshaw," said Goethe, laughing, "as if love had anything to do with the understanding. The things that we love in a young lady are something very different from the understanding. We love in her beauty, youthfulness, playfulness, trustingness, her character, her faults, her caprices, and God knows what *'je ne sais quoi'* besides; but we do not *love* her understanding. We respect her understanding when it is brilliant, and by it the worth of a girl can be infinitely enhanced in our eyes. Understanding may also serve to fix our affections when we already love; but the understanding is not that which is capable of firing our hearts, and awakening a passion."

We found much that was true and convincing in Goethe's words, and were very willing to consider the subject in that light. After dinner, and when the rest of the party had departed, I remained sitting with Goethe, and conversed with him on various interesting topics.

We discoursed upon English literature, on the greatness of Shakespeare, and on the unfavorable position held by all English dramatic authors who had appeared after that poetical giant.

"A dramatic talent of any importance," said Goethe, "could not forbear to notice Shakespeare's works, nay, could not forbear to study them. Having studied them, he must be aware that Shakespeare has already exhausted the whole of human nature in all its tendencies, in all its heights and depths, and that, in fact, there remains for him, the aftercomer, nothing more to do. And how could one get courage only to put pen to paper, if one were conscious in an earnest, appreciating spirit, that such unfathomable and unattainable excellences were already in existence!

"It fared better with me fifty years ago in my own dear Germany. I could soon come to an end with all that then existed; it could not long awe me, or occupy my attention. I soon left behind me German literature, and the study of it, and turned my thoughts to life and to production. So on and on I went in my own natural development, and on and on I fashioned the productions of epoch after epoch. And at every step of life and development, my standard of excellence was not much higher than what at such step I was able to attain. But had I been born an Englishman, and had all those numerous masterpieces been brought before me in all their power, at my first dawn of youthful consciousness, they would have overpowered me, and I should not have known what to do. I could not have gone on with such fresh light-heartedness, but should have had to bethink myself, and look about for a long time, to find some new outlet."

I turned the conversation back to Shakespeare. "When one, to some degree, disengages him from English literature," said I, "and considers him transformed into a German, one cannot fail to look upon his gigantic greatness as a miracle. But if one seeks him in his home, transplants oneself to the soil of his country, and to the atmosphere of the century in which he lived; further, if one studies his contemporaries, and his immediate successors, and inhales the force wafted to us from Ben Jonson, Massinger, Marlowe, and Beaumont and Fletcher, Shakespeare still, indeed, appears a being of the most exalted magnitude; but still, one arrives at the conviction that many of the wonders of his genius are, in some measure, accessible, and that much is due to the powerfully productive atmosphere of his age and time."

"You are perfectly right," returned Goethe. "It is with Shakespeare as with the mountains of Switzerland. Transplant Mont Blanc at once into the large plain of Lüneburg Heath, and we should find no words to express our wonder at its magnitude. Seek it, however, in its gigantic home, go to it over its immense neighbors, the Jungfrau, the Finsteraarhorn, the Eiger, the Wetterhorn, St. Gotthard, and Monte Rosa; Mont Blanc will, indeed, still remain a giant, but it will no longer produce in us such amazement."

"Besides, let him who will not believe," continued Goethe, "that much of Shakespeare's greatness appertains to his great vigorous time, only ask himself the question, whether a phenomenon so astounding would be possible in the present England of 1824, in these evil days of criticising and hair-splitting journals?"

"That undisturbed, innocent, somnambulatory production, by which alone anything great can thrive, is no longer possible. Our talents at present lie before the public. The daily criticisms which appear in fifty different places, and the gossip that is caused by them amongst the public, prevent the appearance of any sound production. In the present day, he who does not keep aloof from all this, and isolate himself by main force, is lost. Through the bad, chiefly negative, æsthetical and critical tone of the journals, a sort of half culture finds its way into the masses; but to productive talent it is a noxious mist, a dropping poison, which destroys the tree of creative power, from the ornamental green leaves, to the deepest pith and the most hidden fibres.

"And then how tame and weak has life itself become during the last two shabby centuries. Where do we now meet an original nature? and where is the man who has the strength to be true, and to show himself as he is? This, however, affects the poet, who must find all within himself, while he is left in the lurch by all without."

The conversation now turned on *Werthe*. "That," said Goethe, "is a creation which I, like the pelican, fed with the blood of my own heart. It contains so much from the innermost recesses of my breast—so much feeling and thought, that it might easily be spread into a novel of ten such volumes. Besides, as I have often said, I have only read the book once since its appearance, and have taken good care not to read it again. It is a mass of congreve-rockets. I am uncomfortable when I look at it; and I dread lest I should once more experience the peculiar mental state from which it was produced."

I reminded him of his conversation with Napoleon, of which I knew by the sketch amongst his unpublished papers, which I had repeatedly urged him to give more in detail. "Napoleon," said I, "pointed out to you a passage in *Werther*, which, it appeared to him, would not stand a strict examination; and this you allowed. I should much like to know what passage he meant."

"Guess!" said Goethe, with a mysterious smile.

"Now," said I, "I almost think it is where Charlotte sends the pistols to Werther, without saying a word to Albert, and without imparting to him her misgivings and apprehensions. You have given yourself great trouble to find a motive for this silence, but it does not appear to hold good against the urgent necessity where the life of the friend was at stake."

"Your remark," returned Goethe, "is really not bad; but I do not think it right to reveal whether Napoleon meant this passage or another. However, be that as it may, your observation is quite as correct as his."

I asked the question, whether the great effect produced by the appearance of *Werther* was really to be attributed to the period. "I cannot," said I, "reconcile to myself this view, though it is so extensively spread. *Werther* made an epoch because it appeared—not because it appeared at a certain time. There is in every period so much unexpressed sorrow—so much secret discontent and disgust for life, and, in single individuals, there are so many disagreements with the world—so many conflicts between their natures and civil regulations, that *Werther* would make an epoch even if it appeared today for the first time."

"You are quite right," said Goethe; "it is on that account that the book to this day influences youth of a certain age, as it did formerly. It was scarcely necessary for me to deduce my own youthful dejection from the general influence of my time, and from the reading of a few English authors. Rather was it owing to individual and immediate circumstances which touched me to the quick, and gave me a great deal of trouble, and indeed brought me into that frame of mind which produced *Werther*. I had lived, loved, and suffered much—that was it."

"On considering more closely the much-talked-of *Werther* period, we discover that it does not belong to the course of universal culture, but to the career of life in every individual, who, with an innate free natural instinct, must accommodate himself to the narrow limits of an antiquated world. Obstructed fortune, restrained activity, unfulfilled wishes, are not the calamities of any particular time, but those of every individual man; and it would be bad, indeed, if every one had not, once in his life, known a time when Werther seemed as if it had been written for him alone."

Sunday, January 4.—Today, after dinner, Goethe went through a portfolio, containing some works of Raphael, with me. He often busies himself with Raphael, in order to keep up a constant intercourse with that which is best, and to accustom himself to muse upon the thoughts of a great man. At the same time, it gives him pleasure to introduce me to such things.

We afterwards spoke about the *Divan*[4]—especially about the "book of ill-humor," in which much is poured forth that he carried in his heart against his enemies.

"If I have, however," continued he, "been very moderate: if I had uttered all that vexed me or gave me trouble, the few pages would soon have swelled to a volume.

"People were never thoroughly contented with me, but always wished me otherwise than it has pleased God to make me. They were also seldom contented with my productions. When I had long exerted my whole soul to favor the world with a new work, it still desired that I should thank it into the bargain for considering the work endurable. If any one praised me, I was not allowed, in self-congratulation, to receive it as a well-merited tribute; but people expected from me some

[4] Goethe's "West-östliche (west-eastern) Divan," one of the twelve divisions of which is entitled "Das Buch des Unmuths" (The Book of Ill-Humor).—Trans.

modest expression, humbly setting forth the total unworthiness of my person and my work. However, my nature opposed this; and I should have been a miserable hypocrite, if I had so tried to lie and dissemble. Since I was strong enough to show myself in my whole truth, just as I felt, I was deemed proud, and am considered so to the present day.

"In religious, scientific, and political matters, I generally brought trouble upon myself, because I was no hypocrite, and had the courage to express what I felt.

"I believed in God and in Nature, and in the triumphs of good over evil; but this was not enough for pious souls; I was also required to believe other points, which were opposed to the feeling of my soul for truth; besides, I did not see that these would be of the slightest service to me.

"It was also prejudicial to me that I discovered Newton's theory of light and color to be an error, and that I had the courage to contradict the universal creed. I discovered light in its purity and truth, and I considered it my duty to fight for it. The opposite party, however, did their utmost to darken the light; for they maintained that *shade is a part of light*. It sounds absurd when I express it; but so it is: for they said that *colors*, which are shadow and the result of shade, *are light itself*, or, which amounts to the same thing, *are the beams of light, broken now in one way, now in another*."

Goethe was silent, whilst an ironical smile spread over his expressive countenance. He continued—

"And now for political matters. What trouble I have taken, and what I have suffered, on that account, I cannot tell you. Do you know my 'Aufgeregten?'"[5]

"Yesterday, for the first time," returned I, "I read the piece, in consequence of the new edition of your works; and I regret from my heart that it remains unfinished. But, even as it is, every right-thinking person must coincide with your sentiments."

"I wrote it at the time of the French Revolution," continued Goethe, "and it may be regarded, in some measure, as my political confession of faith at that time. I have taken the countess as a type of the nobility; and, with the words which I put into her mouth, I have expressed how the nobility really ought to think. The countess has just returned from Paris; she has there been an eye-witness of the revolutionary events, and has drawn, therefore, for herself, no bad doctrine. She has convinced herself that the people may be ruled, but not oppressed, and that the revolutionary outbreaks of the lower classes are the consequence of the injustice of the higher classes. 'I will for the future,' says she, 'strenuously avoid every action that appears to me unjust, and will, both in society and at court, loudly express my opinion concerning such actions in others. In no case of injustice will I be silent, even though I should be cried down as a democrat.'

"I should have thought this sentiment perfectly respectable," continued Goethe; "it was mine at that time, and it is so still; but as a reward for it, I was

---

[5] *Die Aufgeregten* (the Agitated, in a political sense) is an unfinished drama by Goethe.—Trans.

endowed with all sorts of titles, which I do not care to repeat."

"One need only read *Egmont*," answered I, "to discover what you think. I know no German piece in which the freedom of the people is more advocated than in this."

"Sometimes," said Goethe, "people do not like to look on me as I am, but turn their glances from everything which could show me in my true light. Schiller, on the contrary—who, between ourselves, was much more of an aristocrat than I am, but who considered what he said more than I—had the wonderful fortune to be looked upon as a particular friend of the people. I give it up to him with all my heart, and console myself with the thought that others before me had fared no better.

"It is true that I could be no friend to the French Revolution; for its horrors were too near me, and shocked me daily and hourly, whilst its beneficial results were not then to be discovered. Neither could I be indifferent to the fact that the Germans were endeavoring, artificially, to bring about such scenes here, as were, in France, the consequence of a great necessity.

"But I was as little a friend to arbitrary rule. Indeed, I was perfectly convinced that a great revolution is never a fault of the people, but of the government. Revolutions are utterly impossible as long as governments are constantly just and constantly vigilant, so that they may anticipate them by improvements at the right time, and not hold out until they are forced to yield by the pressure from beneath.

"Because I hated the Revolution, the name of the '*Friend of the powers that be*' was bestowed upon me. That is, however, a very ambiguous title, which I would beg to decline. If the 'powers that be' were all that is excellent, good, and just, I should have no objection to the title; but, since with much that is good there is also much that is bad, unjust, and imperfect, a friend of the 'powers that be' means often little less than the friend of the obsolete and bad.[6]

"But time is constantly progressing, and human affairs wear every fifty years a different aspect; so that an arrangement which, in the year 1800, was perfection, may, perhaps, in the year 1850, be a defect.

"And, furthermore, nothing is good for a nation but that which arises from its own core and its own general wants, without apish imitation of another; since what to one race of people, of a certain age, is a wholesome nutriment, may perhaps prove a poison for another. All endeavors to introduce any foreign innovation, the necessity for which is not rooted in the core of the nation itself, are therefore foolish; and all premeditated revolutions of the kind are I unsuccessful, *for they are without God, who keeps aloof from such bungling*. If, however, there exists an actual necessity for a great reform amongst a people, God is with it, and it prospers. He was visibly with Christ and his first adherents; for the appearance of the new doctrine of love was a necessity to the people. He was also visibly with

---

[6] The German phrase "Freund des Bestehenden," which, for want of a better expression, has been rendered above "friend of the powers that be," literally means "friend of the permanent," and was used by the detractors of Goethe to denote the "enemy of the progressive."—*Trans.*

Luther; for the purification of the doctrine corrupted by the priests was no less a necessity. Neither of the great powers whom I have named was, however, a friend of the permanent; much more were both of them convinced that the old leaven must be got rid of, and that it would be impossible to go on and remain in the untrue, unjust, and defective way."

Tuesday, January 27.—Goethe talked with me about the continuation of his memoirs, with which he is now busy. He observed that this later period of his life would not be narrated with such minuteness as the youthful epoch of *Dichtung and Wahrheit*.[7] "I must," said he, "treat this later period more in the fashion of annals: my outward actions must appear rather than my inward life. Altogether, the most important part of an individual's life is that of development, and mine is concluded in the detailed volumes of *Dichtung and Wahrheit*. Afterwards begins the conflict with the world, and that is interesting only in its results.

"And then the life of a learned German—what is it? What may have been really good in my case cannot be communicated, and what can be communicated is not worth the trouble. Besides, where are the hearers whom one could entertain with any satisfaction?

"When I look back to the earlier and middle periods of my life, and now in my old age think how few are left of those who were young with me, I always think of a summer residence at a bathing-place. When you arrive, you make acquaintance and friends of those who have already been there some time, and who leave in a few weeks. The loss is painful. Then you turn to the second generation, with which you live a good while, and become most intimate. But this goes also, and leaves us alone with the third, which comes just as we are going away, and with which we have, properly, nothing to do.

"I have ever been esteemed one of Fortune's chiefest favorites; nor will I complain or find fault with the course my life has taken. Yet, truly, there has been nothing but toil and care; and I may say that, in all my seventy-five years, I have never had a month of genuine comfort. It has been the perpetual rolling of a stone, which I have always had to raise anew. My annals will render clear what I now say. The claims upon my activity, both from within and without, were too numerous.

"My real happiness was my poetic meditation and production. But how was this disturbed, limited, and hindered by my external position! Had I been able to abstain more from public business, and to live more in solitude, I should have been happier, and should have accomplished much more as a poet. But, soon after my *Goetz and Werther*, that saying of a sage was verified for me—'If you do anything for the sake of the world, it will take good care that you shall not do it a second time.'

"A wide-spread celebrity, an elevated position in life, are good things. But, for all my rank and celebrity, I am still obliged to be silent as to the opinion of others, that I may not give offense. This would be but poor sport, if by this means I had not the advantage of learning the thoughts of others without their being able to learn mine."

---

[7] Poetry and Truth, the title of Goethe's autobiography.—Trans.

* * * * *

Wednesday, February 25.—Today, Goethe showed me two very remarkable poems, both highly moral in their tendency, but in their several motives so unreservedly natural and true, that they are of the kind which the world styles immoral. On this account he keeps them to himself, and does not intend to publish them.

"Could intellect and high cultivation," said he, "become the property of all, the poet would have fair play; he could be always thoroughly true, and would not be compelled to fear uttering his best thoughts. But, as it is, he must always keep on a certain level; must remember that his works will fall into the hands of a mixed society; and must, therefore, take care lest by over-great openness he may give offense to the majority of good men. Then Time is a strange thing. It is a whimsical tyrant, which in every century has a different face for all that one says and does. We cannot, with propriety, say things which were permitted to the ancient Greeks; and the Englishmen of 1820 cannot endure what suited the vigorous contemporaries of Shakespeare; so that, at the present day, it is found necessary to have a Family Shakespeare."

"Then," said I, "there is much in the form also. The one of these two poems, which is composed in the style and metre of the ancients, would be far less offensive than the other. Isolated parts would displease, but the treatment throws so much grandeur and dignity over the whole, that we seem to hear a strong ancient, and to be carried back to the age of the Greek heroes. But the other, being in the style and metre of Messer Ariosto, is far more hazardous. It relates an event of our day, in the language of our day, and as it thus comes quite unveiled into our presence, the particular features of boldness seem far more audacious."

"You are right," said he; "mysterious and great effects are produced by different poetical forms. If the import of my Romish elegies were put into the measure and style of Byron's *Don Juan*, the whole would be found infamous."

The French newspapers were brought. The campaign of the French in Spain under the Duke d'Angoulême, which was just ended, had great interest for Goethe. "I must praise the Bourbons for this measure," said he; "they had not really gained the throne till they had gained the army, and that is now accomplished. The soldier returns with loyalty, to his king; for he has, from his own victories, and the discomfitures of the many-headed Spanish host, learned the difference between obeying one and many. The army has sustained its ancient fame, and shown that it is brave in itself, and can conquer without Napoleon."

Goethe then turned his thoughts backward into history, and talked much of the Prussian army in the Seven Years' War, which, accustomed by Frederic the Great to constant victory, grew careless, so that, in after days, it lost many battles from over-confidence. All the minutest details were present to his mind, and I had reason to admire his excellent memory.

"I had the great advantage," said he, "of being born at a time when the greatest events which agitated the world occurred, and such have continued to occur during my long life; so that I am a living witness of the Seven Years' War, of the separation of America from England, of the French Revolution, and of the whole

Napoleon era, with the downfall of that hero, and the events which followed. Thus I have attained results and insight impossible to those who are born now and must learn all these things from books which they will not understand.

"What the next years will bring I cannot predict; but I fear we shall not soon have repose. It is not given to the world to be contented; the great are not such that there will be no abuse of power; the masses not such that, in hope of gradual improvement, they will be contented with a moderate condition. Could we perfect human nature, we might also expect a perfect state of things; but, as it is, there will always be a wavering hither and thither; one part must suffer while the other is at ease, envy and egotism will be always at work like bad demons, and party strife will be without end.

"The most reasonable way is for every one to follow his own vocation to which he has been born, and which he has learned, and to avoid hindering others from following theirs. Let the shoemaker abide by his last, the peasant by his plough, and let the king know how to govern; for, this is also a business which must be learned, and with which no one should meddle who does not understand it."

Returning to the French papers, Goethe said: "The liberals may speak, for when they are reasonable we like to hear them; but with the royalists, who have the executive power in their hands, talking comes amiss—they should act. They may march troops, and behead and hang—that is all right; but attacking opinions, and justifying their measures in public prints, does not become them. If there were a public of kings, they might talk.

"For myself," he continued, "I have always been a royalist. I have let others babble, and have done as I saw fit. I understood my course, and knew my own object. If I committed a fault as a single individual, I could make it good again; but if I committed it jointly with three or four others, it would be impossible to make it good, for among many there are many opinions."

Goethe was in excellent spirits today. He showed me Frau von Spiegel's album, in which he had written some very beautiful verses. A place had been left open for him for two years, and he rejoiced at having been able to perform at last an old promise. After I had read the "Poem to Frau von Spiegel," I turned over the leaves of the book, in which I found many distinguished names. On the very next page was a poem by Tiedge, written in the very spirit and style of his *Urania*. "In a saucy mood," said Goethe, "I was on the point of writing some verses beneath those; but I am glad I did not. It would not have been the first time that, by rash expressions, I had repelled good people, and spoiled the effect of my best works.

"However," continued Goethe, "I have had to endure not a little from Tiedge's *Urania*; for, at one time, nothing was sung and nothing was declaimed but this same Urania. Wherever you went, you found *Urania* on the table. *Urania* and immortality were the topics of every conversation. I would by no means dispense with the happiness of believing in a future existence, and, indeed, would say, with Lorenzo de' Medici, that those are dead even for this life who hope for no other. But such incomprehensible matters lie too far off to be a theme of daily meditation and thought-distracting speculation. Let him who believes in immortality enjoy his happiness in silence, he has no reason to give himself airs about it. The occasion of Tiedge's *Urania* led me to observe that piety, like nobility, has its aristocracy. I met stupid women, who plumed themselves on believing, with Tiedge, in immortality, and I was forced to bear much dark examination on this point. They were vexed by my saying I should be well pleased if, after the close of this life, we were blessed with another, only I hoped I should hereafter meet none of those who had believed in it here. For how should I be tormented! The pious would throng around me, and say, 'Were we not right? Did we not predict it? Has not it happened just as we said?' And so there would be ennui without end, even in the other world.

"This occupation with the ideas of immortality," he continued, "is for people of rank, and especially ladies, who have nothing to do. But an able man, who has some thing regular to do here, and must toil and struggle and produce day by day, leaves the future world to itself, and is active and useful in this. Thoughts about immortality are also good for those who have not been very successful here; and I would wager that, if the good Tiedge had enjoyed a better lot, he would also have had better thoughts."

* * * * *

Tuesday, November 9.—I passed this evening with Goethe. We talked of Klopstock and Herder; and I liked to listen to him, as he explained to me the merits of those men.

"Without those powerful precursors," said Goethe, "our literature could not have become what it now is. When they appeared, they were before their age, and were obliged, as it were, to drag it after them; but now the age has far outrun them, and they who were once so necessary and important have now ceased to be *means to an end*. A young man who would take Klopstock and Herder for his teachers nowadays would be far behindhand."

We talked over Klopstock's *Messiah* and his Odes, touching on their merits and their defects. We agreed that he had no faculty for observing and apprehending the visible world, or for drawing characters; and that he therefore wanted the qualities most essential to the epic and dramatic poet, or, perhaps it might be said, to the poet generally.

"An ode occurs to me," said Goethe, "where he makes the German Muse run a race with the British; and, indeed, when one thinks what a picture it is, where the two girls run one against the other, throwing about their legs and kicking up the dust, one must assume that the good Klopstock did not really have before his eyes such pictures as he wrote, else he could not possibly have made such mistakes."

I asked how he had felt towards Klopstock in his youth. "I venerated him," said Goethe, "with the devotion which was peculiar to me; I looked upon him as my uncle. I revered whatever he had done, and never thought of reflecting upon it, or finding fault with it. I let his fine qualities work upon me; for the rest, I went my own way."

We came back to Herder, and I asked Goethe which of his works he thought the best. *"His Idea for the History of Mankind"* (*Ideen zur Geschichte der Menschheit*), replied Goethe, "are undoubtedly the best. In after days, he took the negative side, and was not so agreeable."

"Considering the great weight of Herder," said I, "I cannot understand how he had so little judgment on some subjects. For instance, I cannot forgive him, especially at that period of German literature, for sending back the manuscript of *Goetz von Berlichingen* without any praise of its merits, and with taunting remarks. He must have utterly wanted organs to perceive some objects."

"Yes, Herder was unfortunate in this respect," replied Goethe; "nay," added he, with vivacity, "if his spirit were present at this conversation, it would not understand us."

"On the other hand," said I, "I must praise Merck, who urged you to print *Goetz*."

"He was indeed an odd but important man," said Goethe. "'Print the thing,' quoth he, 'it is worth nothing, but print it.' He did not wish me to make any alteration in it, and he was right; for it would have been different, but not better."

Wednesday, November 24.—I went to see Goethe this evening, before going to the theatre, and found him very well and cheerful. He inquired about the young Englishmen who are here. I told him that I proposed reading with Mr. Doolan a German translation of Plutarch. This led the conversation to Roman and Grecian history; and Goethe expressed himself as follows:

"The Roman history," said he, "is no longer suited to us. We have become too humane for the triumphs of Cæsar not to be repugnant to our feelings. Neither are we much charmed by the history of Greece. When this people turns against a foreign foe, it is, indeed, great and glorious; but the division of the states, and their eternal wars with one another, where Greek fights against Greek, are insufferable. Besides, the history of our own time is thoroughly great and important; the battles of Leipsic and Waterloo stand out with such prominence that that of Marathon and others like it are gradually eclipsed. Neither are our individual heroes inferior to theirs; the French Marshals, Blücher, and Wellington, vie with any of the heroes of antiquity."

We then talked of the late French literature, and the daily increasing interest in German works manifested by the French.

"The French," said Goethe, "do well to study and translate our writers; for, limited as they are both in form and motives, they can only look without for means. We Germans may be reproached for a certain formlessness; but in matter we are their superiors. The theatrical productions of Kotzebue and Iffland are so rich in motives that they may pluck them a long time before all is used up. But, especially, our philosophical Ideality is welcome to them; for every Ideal is serviceable to revolutionary aims.

"The French have understanding and *esprit*, but neither a solid basis nor piety. What serves the moment, what helps his party, seems right to the Frenchman. Hence they praise us, never from an acknowledgment of our merits, but only when they can strengthen their party by our views."

We then talked about our own literature, and of the obstacles in the way of some of our latest young poets.

"The majority of our young poets," said Goethe, "have no fault but this, that their subjectivity is not important, and that they cannot find matter in the objective. At best, they only find a material, which is similar to themselves, which corresponds to their own subjectivity; but as for taking the material on its own account, when it is repugnant to the subjectivity, merely because it is poetical, such a thing is never thought of.

"Still, as I have said, if we only had important personages, formed by great studies and situations in life, it might still go well with us, at least as far as our young lyric poets are concerned."

1825

Monday, January 10.—Goethe, consistently with his great interest for the English, has desired me to introduce to him the young Englishmen who are here at present.

After we had waited a few minutes, Goethe came in, and greeted us cordially. He said to Mr. H., "I presume I may address you in German, as I hear you are already well versed in our language." Mr. H. answered with a few polite words, and Goethe requested us to be seated.

Mr. H.'s manners and appearance must have made a good impression on Goethe; for his sweetness and mild serenity were manifested towards the stranger in their real beauty. "You did well," said he "to come hither to learn German; for here you will quickly and easily acquire, not only a knowledge of the language, but also of the elements on which it rests, our soil, climate, mode of life, manners, social habits, and constitution, and carry it away with you to England."

Mr. H. replied, "The interest taken in the German language is now great, so that there is now scarcely a young Englishman of good family who does not learn German."

"We Germans," said Goethe, good-humoredly, "have, however, been half a century before your nation in this respect. For fifty years I have been busy with the English language and literature; so that I am well acquainted with your writers, your ways of living, and the administration of your country. If I went over to England, I should be no stranger there.

"But, as I said before, your young men do well to come to us and learn our language; for, not only does our literature merit attention on its own account, but no one can deny that he who now knows German well can dispense with many other languages. Of the French, I do not speak; it is the language of conversation, and is indispensable in traveling, because everybody understands it, and in all countries we can get on with it instead of a good interpreter. But as for Greek, Latin, Italian, and Spanish, we can read the best works of those nations in such excellent German translations, that, unless we have some particular object in view, we need not spend much time upon the toilsome study of those languages. It is in the German nature duly to honor, after its kind, everything produced by other nations, and to accommodate itself to foreign peculiarities. This, with the great flexibility of our language, makes German translations thoroughly faithful and complete. And it is not to be denied that, in general, you get on very far with a good translation. Frederick the Great did not know Latin, but he read Cicero in the French translation with as much profit as we who read him in the original."

Then, turning the conversation on the theatre, he asked Mr. H. whether he went frequently thither. "Every evening," he replied, "and find that I thus gain much towards the understanding of the language."

"It is remarkable," said Goethe, "that the ear, and generally the understanding, gets the start of speaking; so that a man may very soon comprehend all he hears, but by no means express it all."

"I experience daily," said Mr. H., "the truth of that remark. I understand very well whatever I hear or read; I even feel when an incorrect expression is made use of in German. But when I speak, nothing will flow, and I cannot express myself as I wish. In light conversation at court, jests with the ladies, a chat at balls, and the like, I succeed pretty well. But, if I try to express an opinion on any important topic, to say anything peculiar or luminous, I cannot get on."

"Be not discouraged by that," said Goethe, "since it is hard enough to express such uncommon matters in one's own mother tongue."

He then asked what Mr. H. read in German literature. "I have read *Egmont*," he replied, "and found so much pleasure in the perusal that I returned to it three times. *Torquato Tasso*, too, has afforded me much enjoyment. Now I am reading *Faust*, but find that it is somewhat difficult."

Goethe laughed at these last words. "Really," said he, "I would not have advised you to undertake *Faust*. It is mad stuff, and goes quite beyond all ordinary feeling. But since you have done it of your own accord, without asking my advice, you will see how you will get through. Faust is so strange an individual that only few can sympathize with his internal condition. Then the character of Mephistopheles is, on account of his irony, and also because he is a living result of an extensive acquaintance with the world, also very difficult. But you will see what lights open upon you. *Tasso*, on the other hand, lies far nearer the common feelings of mankind, and the elaboration of its form is favorable to an easy comprehension of it."

"Yet," said Mr. H., "*Tasso* is thought difficult in Germany, and people have wondered to hear me say that I was reading it."

"What is chiefly needed for *Tasso*," replied Goethe, "is that one should be no longer a child, and should have been in good society. A young man of good family, with sufficient mind and delicacy, and also with enough outward culture, such as will be produced by intercourse with accomplished men of the higher class, will not find' Tasso difficult."

The conversation turning upon *Egmont*, he said, "I wrote *Egmont* in 1775 — fifty years ago. I adhered closely to history, and strove to be as accurate as possible. Ten years afterwards, when I was in Rome, I read in the newspapers that the revolutionary scenes in the Nether lands there described were exactly repeated. I saw from this that the world remains ever the same, and that my picture must have some life in it."

Amid this and similar conversation, the hour for the theatre had come. We arose, and Goethe dismissed us in a friendly manner.

As we went homeward, I asked Mr. H. how he was pleased with Goethe. "I have never," said he, "seen a man who, with all his attractive gentleness, had so much native dignity. However he may condescend, he is always the great man."

Professor Riemer was announced, Rehbein took leave, and Riemer sat down with us. The conversation still turned on the *motives* of the Servian love-poems. Riemer was acquainted with the topic, and made the remark that, according to the table of contents given above, not only could poems be made, but that the same motives had been already used by the Germans, without any knowledge that they had been treated in Servia. He mentioned some poems of his own, and I mentioned some poems by Goethe, which had occurred to me during the reading.

"The world," said Goethe, "remains always the same; situations are repeated; one people lives, loves, and feels like another; why should not one poet write like another? The situations of life are alike; why, then, should those of poems be unlike?"

"This very similarity in life and sensation," said Riemer, "makes us all able to appreciate the poetry of other nations. If this were not the case, we should never know what foreign poems were about."

"I am, therefore," said I, "always surprised at the learned, who seem to suppose that poetizing proceeds not from life to the poem, but from the book to the poem. They are always saying, 'He got this here; he got that there.' If, for instance, they find passages in Shakespeare which are also to be found in the ancients, they say he must have taken them from the ancients. Thus there is a situation in Shakespeare, where, on the sight of a beautiful girl, the parents are congratulated who call her daughter, and the youth who will lead her home as his bride. And because the same thing occurs in Homer, Shakespeare, forsooth, has taken it from Homer. How odd! As if one had to go so far for such things, and did not have them before one's eyes, feel them and utter them every day." "Ah, yes," said Goethe, "it is very ridiculous."

"Lord Byron, too," said I, "is no wiser, when he takes *Faust* to pieces, and thinks you found one thing here, the other there."

"The greater part of those fine things cited by Lord Byron," said Goethe, "I have never even read, much less did I think of them, when I was writing *Faust*. But Lord Byron is great only as a poet; as soon as he reflects, he is a child. He knows not how to help himself against the stupid attacks of the same kind made upon him by his own countrymen. He ought to have expressed himself more strongly against them. 'What is there is mine,' he should have said, 'and whether I got it from a book or from life, is of no consequence; the only point is, whether I have made a right use of it.' Walter Scott used a scene from my *Egmont*, and he had a right to do so; and because he did it well, he deserves praise. He has also copied the character of my Mignon in one of his romances; but whether with equal judgment, is another question. Lord Byron's transformed Devil[8] is a continuation of Mephistopheles, and quite right too. If, from the whim of originality, he had departed from the model, he would certainly have fared worse. Thus, my Mephistopheles sings a song from Shakespeare, and why should he not? Why should I give myself the trouble of inventing one of my own, when this said just what was wanted. If, too, the prologue to my *Faust* is something like the beginning of Job, that is again quite right, and I am rather to be praised than censured."

Goethe was in the best humor. He sent for a bottle of wine, and filled for Riemer and me; he himself drank Marienbad water. He seemed to have appointed this evening for looking over, with Riemer, the manuscript of the continuation of his autobiography, perhaps in order to improve it here and there, in point of expression. "Let Eckermann stay and hear it too," said Goethe; which words I was very glad to hear, and he then laid the manuscript before Riemer, who began to read, commencing with the year 1795.

I had already, in the course of the summer, had the pleasure of repeatedly reading and reflecting on the still unpublished record of those years, down to the latest time. But now to hear them read aloud in Goethe's presence, afforded quite a new enjoyment. Riemer paid especial attention to the mode of expression; and I had occasion to admire his great dexterity, and his affluence of words and phrases. But in Goethe's mind the epoch of life described was revived; he revelled in recollections, and on the mention of single persons and events, filled out the written narrative by the details he orally gave us. That was a precious evening! The most distinguished of his contemporaries were talked over; but the conversation always came back to Schiller, who was so interwoven with this period, from 1795 to 1800. The theatre had been the object of their united efforts, and Goethe's best works belong to this time. *Wilhelm Meister* was completed; *Hermann and Dorothea* planned and written; *Cellini* translated for the "Horen;" the "Xenien" written by both for Schiller's *Musenalmanach*; every day brought with it points of contact. Of all this we talked this evening, and Goethe had full opportunity for the most interesting communications.

"*Hermann and Dorothea*," said he, "is almost the only one of my larger poems which still satisfies me; I can never read it without strong interest. I love it best in the Latin translation; there it seems to me nobler, and as if it had returned to its original form."

Wilhelm Meister was often a subject of discourse. "Schiller blamed me for interweaving tragic elements which do not belong to the novel. Yet he was wrong, as we all know. In his letters to me, there are most important views and opinions with respect to *Wilhelm Meister*. But this work is one of the most incalculable productions; I myself can scarcely be said to have the key to it. People seek a central point,

[8] This, doubtless, means the "Deformed Transformed," and the fact that this poem was not published till January, 1824, rendering it probable that Goethe had not actually seen it, accounts for the inaccuracy of the expression.—Trans.

and that is hard, and not even right. I should think a rich, manifold life, brought close to our eyes, would be enough in itself, without any express tendency, which, after all, is only for the intellect. But if anything of the sort is insisted upon, it will perhaps be found in the words which Frederic, at the end, addresses to the hero, when he says—'Thou seem'st to me like Saul, the son of Kish, who went out to seek his father's asses, and found a kingdom.' Keep only to this; for, in fact, the whole work seems to say nothing more than that man, despite all his follies and errors, being led by a higher hand, reaches some happy goal at last."

We then talked of the high degree of culture which, during the last fifty years, had become general among the middle classes of Germany, and Goethe ascribed the merit of this not so much to Lessing as to Herder and Wieland. "Lessing," said he, "was of the very highest understanding, and only one equally great could truly learn of him. To a half faculty he was dangerous." He mentioned a journalist who had formed himself on Lessing, and at the end of the last century had played a part indeed, but far from a noble one, because he was so inferior to his great predecessor.

"All Upper Germany," said he, "is indebted to Wieland for its style. It has learned much from him; and the capability of expressing itself correctly is not the least."

On mentioning the *Xenien*,[9] he especially praised those of Schiller, which he called sharp and biting, while he called his own innocent and trivial.

"The *Thierkreis* (Zodiac), which is by Schiller," said he, "I always read with admiration. The good effects which the *Xenien* had upon the German literature of their time are beyond calculation." Many persons against whom the *Xenien* were directed, were mentioned on this occasion, but their names have escaped my memory.

After we had read and talked over the manuscript to the end of the year 1800, interrupted by these and innumerable other observations from Goethe, he put aside the papers, and had a little supper placed at one end of the table at which we were sitting. We partook of it, but Goethe did not touch a morsel; indeed, I have never seen him eat in the evening. He sat down with us, filled our glasses, snuffed the candles, and intellectually regaled us with the most agreeable conversation. His remembrance of Schiller was so lively, that the conversation during the latter part of the evening was devoted to him alone.

Riemer spoke of Schiller's personal appearance. "The build of his limbs, his gait in the street, all his motions," said he, "were proud; his eyes only were soft."

"Yes," said Goethe, "everything else about him was proud and majestic, only the eyes were soft. And his talent was like his outward form. He seized boldly on a great subject, and turned it this way and that, and handled it this way and that. But he saw his object, as it were, only in the outside; a quiet development from its interior was not within his province. His talent was desultory. Thus he was never decided—could never have done. He often changed a part just before a rehearsal.

[9] It need scarcely be mentioned that this is the name given to a collection of sarcastic epigrams by Goethe and Schiller.—Trans.

"And, as he went so boldly to work, he did not take sufficient pains about *motives*. I recollect what trouble I had with him, when he wanted to make Gessler, in Tell, abruptly break an apple from the tree, and have it shot from the boy's head. This was quite against my nature, and I urged him to give at least some motive to this barbarity, by making the boy boast to Gessler of his father's dexterity, and say that he could shoot an apple from a tree at a hundred paces. Schiller, at first, would have nothing of the sort: but at last he yielded to my arguments and intentions, and did as I advised him. I, on the other hand, by too great attention to *motives*, kept my pieces from the theatre. My *Eugenie*[10] is nothing but a chain of *motives*, and this cannot succeed on the stage.

"Schiller's genius was really made for the theatre. With every piece he progressed, and became more finished; but, strange to say, a certain love for the horrible adhered to him from the time of *The Robbers*, which never quite left him even in his prime. I still recollect perfectly well, that in the prison scene in my 'Egmont,' where the sentence is read to him, Schiller would have made Alva appear in the background, masked and muffled in a cloak, enjoying the effect which the sentence would produce on Egmont. Thus Alva was to show himself insatiable in revenge and malice. I, however, protested, and prevented the apparition. He was a great, odd man.

"Every week he became different and more finished; each time that I saw him, he seemed to me to have advanced in learning and judgment. His letters are the fairest memorials of him which I possess, and they are also among the most excellent of his writings. His last letter I preserve as a sacred relic, among my treasures." He rose and fetched it. "See and read it," said he; giving it to me.

It was a very fine letter, written in a bold hand. It contained an opinion of Goethe's notes to "Rameau's Nephew," which exhibit French literature at that time, and which he had given Schiller to look over. I read the letter aloud to Riemer.

"You see," said Goethe, "how apt and consistent is his judgment, and that the handwriting nowhere betrays any trace of weakness. He was a splendid man, and went from us in all the fulness of his strength. This letter is dated the 24th of April, 1805. Schiller died on the 9th of May."

We looked at the letter by turns, and were pleased both with the clear style and the fine handwriting. Goethe bestowed several other words of affectionate reminiscence upon his friend, until it was nearly eleven o'clock, and we departed.

* * * * *

Wednesday, October 15. — I found Goethe in a very elevated mood this evening, and had the pleasure of hearing from him many significant remarks. We talked about the state of the newest literature, when Goethe expressed himself as follows:

"Deficiency of character in individual investigators and writers is," he said, "the source of all the evils of our newest literature.

"In criticism, especially, this defect produces mischief to the world, for it either diffuses the false instead of the true, or by a pitiful truth deprives us of some-

[10] "Die Natürliche Tochter" (the Natural Daughter). — *Trans.*

thing great, that would be better.

"Till lately, the world believed in the heroism of a Lucretia—of a Mucius Scævola—and suffered itself, by this belief, to be warmed and inspired. But now comes your historical criticism, and says that those persons never lived, but are to be regarded as fables and fictions, divined by the great mind of the Romans. What are we to do with so pitiful a truth? If the Romans were great enough to invent such stories, we should at least be great enough to believe them.

"Till lately, I was always pleased with a great fact in the thirteenth century, when the Emperor Frederic the Second was at variance with the Pope, and the north of Germany was open to all sorts of hostile attacks. Asiatic hordes had actually penetrated as far as Silesia, when the Duke of Liegnitz terrified them by one great defeat. They then turned to Moravia, but were here defeated by Count Sternberg. These valiant men had on this account been living in my heart as the great saviors of the German nation. But now comes historical criticism, and says that these heroes sacrificed themselves quite uselessly, as the Asiatic army was already recalled, and would have returned of its own accord. Thus is a great national fact crippled and destroyed, which seems to me most abominable."

After these remarks on historical critics, Goethe spoke of another class of seekers and literary men.

"I could never," said he, "have known so well how paltry men are, and how little they care for really high aims, if I had not tested them by my scientific researches. Thus I saw that most men care for science only so far as they get a living by it, and that they worship even error when it affords them a subsistence.

"In *belles lettres* it is no better. There, too, high aims and genuine love for the true and sound, and for their diffusion, are very rare phenomena. One man cherishes and tolerates another, because he is by him cherished and tolerated in return. True greatness is hateful to them; they would fain drive it from the world, so that only such as they might be of importance in it. Such are the masses; and the prominent individuals are not better.

"— — 's great talents and world-embracing learning might have done much for his country. But his want of character has deprived the world of such great results, and himself of the esteem of the country.

"We want a man like Lessing. For how was he great, except in character—in firmness? There are many men as clever and as cultivated, but where is such character?

"Many are full of *esprit* and knowledge, but they are also full of vanity; and that they may shine as wits before the short-sighted multitude, they have no shame or delicacy—nothing is sacred to them.

"Madame de Genlis was therefore perfectly right when she declaimed against the freedoms and profanities of Voltaire. Clever as they all may be, the world has derived no profit from them; they afford a foundation for nothing. Nay, they have been of the greatest injury, since they have confused men and robbed them of their needful support.

"After all, what do we know, and how far can we go with all our wit?

"Man is born not to solve the problems of the universe, but to find out where the problem begins, and then to restrain himself within the limits of the comprehensible.

"His faculties are not sufficient to measure the actions of the universe; and an attempt to explain the outer world by reason is, with his narrow point of view, but a vain endeavor. The reason of man and the reason of the Deity are two very different things.

"If we grant freedom to man, there is an end to the omniscience of God; for if the Divinity knows how I shall act, I must act so perforce. I give this merely as a sign how little we know, and to show that it is not good to meddle with divine mysteries.

"Moreover, we should only utter higher maxims so far as they can benefit the world. The rest we should keep within ourselves, and they will diffuse over our actions a lustre like the mild radiance of a hidden sun."

Sunday, December 25.—"I have of late made an observation, which I will impart to you.

"Everything we do has a result. But that which is right and prudent does not always lead to good, nor the contrary to what is bad; frequently the reverse takes place. Some time since, I made a mistake in one of these transactions with booksellers, and was sorry that I had done so. But now circumstances have so altered, that, if I had not made that very mistake, I should have made a greater one. Such instances occur frequently in life, and hence we see men of the world, who know this, going to work with great freedom and boldness."

I was struck by this remark, which was new to me.

I then turned the conversation to some of his works, and we came to the elegy *Alexis and Dora*.

"In this poem," said Goethe, "people have blamed the strong, passionate conclusion, and would have liked the elegy to end gently and peacefully, without that outbreak of jealousy; but I could not see that they were right. Jealousy is so manifestly an ingredient of the affair, that the poem would be incomplete if it were not introduced at all. I myself knew a young man who, in the midst of his impassioned love for an easily-won maiden, cried out, 'But would she not act to another as she has acted to me?'"

I agreed entirely with Goethe, and then mentioned the peculiar situations in this elegy, where, with so few strokes and in so narrow a space, all is so well delineated that we think we see the whole life and domestic environment of the persons engaged in the action. "What you have described," said I, "appears as true as if you had worked from actual experience."

"I am glad it seems so to you," said Goethe. "There are, however, few men who have imagination for the truth of reality; most prefer strange countries and circumstances, of which they know nothing, and by which their imagination may be cultivated, oddly enough.

"Then there are others who cling altogether to reality, and, as they wholly want the poetic spirit, are too severe in their requisitions. For instance, in this elegy, some would have had me give Alexis a servant to carry his bundle, never thinking that all that was poetic and idyllic in the situation would thus have been destroyed."

From *Alexis and Dora*, the conversation then turned to *Wilhelm Meister*. "There are odd critics in this world," said Goethe; "they blamed me for letting the hero of this novel live so much in bad company; but by this very circumstance that I considered this so-called bad company as a vase into which I could put everything I had to say about good society, I gained a poetical body, and a varied one into the bargain. Had I, on the contrary, delineated good society by the so-called good society, nobody would have read the book.

"In the seeming trivialities of *Wilhelm Meister*, there is always something higher at bottom, and nothing is required but eyes, knowledge of the world, and power of comprehension to perceive the great in the small. For those who are without such qualities, let it suffice to receive the picture of life as real life."

Goethe then showed me a very interesting English work, which illustrated all Shakespeare in copper plates. Each page embraced, in six small designs, one piece with some verses written beneath, so that the leading idea and the most important situations of each work were brought before the eyes. All these immortal tragedies and comedies thus passed before the mind like processions of masks.

"It is even terrifying," said Goethe, "to look through these little pictures. Thus are we first made to feel the infinite wealth and grandeur of Shakespeare. There is no motive in human life which he has not exhibited and expressed! And all with what ease and freedom!

"But we cannot talk about Shakespeare; everything is inadequate. I have touched upon the subject in my *Wilhelm Meister* but that is not saying much. He is not a theatrical poet; he never thought of the stage; it was far too narrow for his great mind: nay, the whole visible world was too narrow.

"He is even too rich and too powerful. A productive *nature*[11] ought not to read more than one of his dramas in a year if it would not be wrecked entirely. I did well to get rid of him by writing *Goetz*, and *Egmont*,[12] and Byron did well by not having too much respect and admiration for him, but going his own way. How many excellent Germans have been ruined by him and Calderon!

"Shakespeare gives us golden apples in silver dishes. We get, indeed, the silver dishes by studying his works; but, unfortunately, we have only potatoes to put into them."

---

[11] Vide p. 185 of "The Greman Classics, Volume II.", where a remark is made on the word *nature*, as applied to a person.—*Trans.*

[12] These plays were intended to be in the Shakesperian style, and Goethe means that by writing them he freed himself from Shakespeare, just as by writing *Werther* he freed himself from thoughts of suicide.—*Trans.*

I laughed, and was delighted with this admirable simile.

Goethe then read me a letter from Zelter, describing a representation of Macbeth at Berlin, where the music could not keep pace with the grand spirit and character of the piece, as Zelter set forth by various intimations. By Goethe's reading, the letter gained its full effect, and he often paused to admire with me the point of some single passage.

"*Macbeth*," said Goethe, "is Shakespeare's best acting play, the one in which he shows most understanding with respect to the stage. But would you see his mind unfettered, read *Troilus and Cressida*, where he treats the materials of the *Iliad* in his own fashion."

The conversation turned upon Byron—the disadvantage in which he appears when placed beside the innocent cheerfulness of Shakespeare, and the frequent and generally not unjust blame which he drew upon himself by his manifold works of negation.

"If Lord Byron," said Goethe, "had had an opportunity of working off all the opposition in his character, by a number of strong parliamentary speeches, he would have been much more pure as a poet. But, as he scarcely ever spoke in parliament, he kept within himself all his feelings against his nation, and to free himself from them, he had no other means than to express them in poetical form. I could, therefore, call a great part of Byron's works of negation 'suppressed parliamentary speeches,' and think this would be no bad name for them."

We then mentioned one of our most modern German poets, Platen, who had lately gained a great name, and whose negative tendency was likewise disapproved. "We cannot deny," said Goethe, "that he has many brilliant qualities, but he is wanting in—love. He loves his readers and his fellow-poets as little as he loves himself, and thus we may apply to him the maxim of the apostle—'Though I speak with the tongues of men and angels, and have not love (charity), I am become as sounding brass and a tinkling cymbal.' I have lately read the poems of Platen, and cannot deny his great talent. But, as I said, he is deficient in *love*, and thus he will never produce the effect which he ought. He will be feared, and will be the idol of those who would like to be as negative as himself, but have not his talent."

* * * * *

1827

Thursday evening, January 18.—The conversation now turned wholly on Schiller, and Goethe proceeded thus: "Schiller's proper productive talent lay in the ideal; and it may be said he has not his equal in German or any other literature. He has almost everything that Lord Byron has; but Lord Byron is his superior in knowledge of the world. I wish Schiller had lived to know Lord Byron's works, and wonder what he would have said to so congenial a mind. Did Byron publish anything during Schiller's life?"

I could not say with certainty. Goethe took down the Conversations Lexicon, and read the article on Byron, making many hasty remarks as he proceeded. It appeared that Byron had published nothing before 1807, and that therefore Schiller could have seen nothing of his.

"Through all Schiller's works," continued Goethe, "goes the idea of freedom; though this idea assumed a new shape as Schiller advanced in his culture and became another man. In his youth it was physical freedom which occupied him, and influenced his poems; in his later life it was ideal freedom.

"Freedom is an odd thing, and every man has enough of it, if he can only satisfy himself. What avails a superfluity of freedom which we cannot use? Look at this chamber and the next, in which, through the open door, you see my bed. Neither of them is large; and they are rendered still narrower by necessary furniture, books, manuscripts, and works of art; but they are enough for me. I have lived in them all the winter, scarcely entering my front rooms. What have I done with my spacious house, and the liberty of going from one room to another, when I have not found it requisite to make use of them?

"If a man has freedom enough to live healthy, and work at his craft, he has enough; and so much all can easily obtain. Then all of us are only free under certain conditions, which we must fulfil. The citizen is as free as the nobleman, when he restrains himself within the limits which God appointed by placing him in that rank. The nobleman is as free as the prince; for, if he will but observe a few ceremonies at court, he may feel himself his equal. Freedom consists not in refusing to recognize anything above us, but in respecting something which is above us; for, by respecting it, we raise ourselves to it, and by our very acknowledgment make manifest that we bear within ourselves what is higher, and are worthy to be on a level with it.

"I have, on my journeys, often met merchants from the north of Germany, who fancied they were my equals, if they rudely seated themselves next me at table. They were, by this method, nothing of the kind; but they would have been so if they had known how to value and treat me.

"That this physical freedom gave Schiller so much trouble in his youthful years, was caused partly by the nature of his mind, but still more by the restraint which he endured at the military school. In later days, when he had enough physical freedom, he passed over to the ideal; and I would almost say that this idea killed him, since it led him to make demands on his physical nature which were too much for his strength.

"The Grand Duke fixed on Schiller, when he was established here, an income of one thousand dollars yearly, and offered to give him twice as much in case he should be hindered by sickness from working. Schiller declined this last offer, and never availed himself of it. 'I have talent,' said he, 'and must help myself.' But as his family enlarged of late years, he was obliged, for a livelihood, to write two dramas annually; and to accomplish this, he forced himself to write days and weeks when he was not well. He would have his talent obey him at any hour. He never drank much; he was very temperate; but, in such hours of bodily weakness, he was obliged to stimulate his powers by the use of spirituous liquors. This habit impaired his health, and was likewise injurious to his productions. The faults which some wiseacres find in his works I deduce from this source. All the passages which they say are not what they ought to be, I would call pathological passages; for he wrote them on those days when he had not strength to find the right and true motives. I have every respect for the categorical imperative. I know how much good may proceed from it; but one must not carry it too far, for then this idea of ideal freedom certainly leads to no good."

Amid these interesting remarks, and similar discourse on Lord Byron and the celebrated German authors, of whom Schiller had said that he liked Kotzebue best, for he, at any rate, produced something, the hours of evening passed swiftly along, and Goethe gave me the novel, that I might study it quietly at home.

* * * * *

Wednesday, February 21.—Dined with Goethe. He spoke much, and with admiration, of Alexander von Humboldt, whose work on Cuba and Colombia he had begun to read and whose views as to the project for making a passage through the Isthmus of Panama appeared to have a particular interest for him. "Humboldt," said Goethe, "has, with a great knowledge of his subject, given other points where, by making use of some streams which flow into the Gulf of Mexico, the end may be perhaps better attained than at Panama. All this is reserved for the future, and for an enterprising spirit. So much, however, is certain, that, if they succeed in cutting such a canal that ships of any burden and size can be navigated through it from the Mexican Gulf to the Pacific Ocean, innumerable benefits would result to the whole human race, civilized and uncivilized. But I should wonder if the United States were to let an opportunity escape of getting such work into their own hands. It may be foreseen that this young state, with its decided predilection to the West, will, in thirty or forty years, have occupied and peopled the large tract of land beyond the Rocky Mountains. It may, furthermore, be foreseen that along the whole coast of the Pacific Ocean, where nature has already formed the most capacious and secure harbors, important commercial towns will gradually arise, for the furtherance of a great intercourse between China and the East Indies and the United States. In such a case, it would not only be desirable, but almost necessary, that a more rapid communication should be maintained between the eastern and western shores of North America, both by merchant-ships and men-of-war, than has hitherto been possible with the tedious, disagreeable, and expensive voyage round Cape Horn. I therefore repeat, that it is absolutely indispensable for the United States to effect a passage from the Mexican Gulf to the Pacific Ocean; and I am certain that they will do it.

"Would that I might live to see it!—but I shall not. I should like to see another thing—a junction of the Danube and the Rhine. But this undertaking is so gigantic that I have doubts of its completion, particularly when I consider our German resources. And thirdly, and lastly, I should wish to see England in possession of a canal through the Isthmus of Suez. Would I could live to see these three great works! it would be well worth the trouble to last some fifty years more for the very purpose."

* * * * *

Thursday, May 3.—The highly successful translation of Goethe's dramatic works, by Stapfer, was noticed by Monsieur J. J. Ampere in the *Parisian Globe* of last year, in a manner no less excellent, and this affected Goethe so agreeably that he very often recurred to it, and expressed his great obligations to it.

"Ampere's point of view is a very high one," said he.

"When German critics on similar occasions start from philosophy, and in the consideration and discussion of a poetical production proceed in a manner that what they intend as an elucidation is only intelligible to philosophers of their own school, while for other people it is far more obscure than the work upon which they intended to throw a light, M. Ampere, on the contrary, shows himself quite practical and popular. Like one who knows his profession thoroughly, he shows the relation between the production and the producer, and judges the different poetical productions as different fruits of different epochs of the poet's life.

"He has studied most profoundly the changing course of my earthly career, and of the condition of my mind, and has had the faculty of seeing what I have not expressed, and what, so to speak, could only be read between the lines. How truly has he remarked that, during the first ten years of my official and court life at Weimar, I scarcely did anything; that despair drove me to Italy; and that I there, with new delight in producing, seized upon the history of Tasso, in order to free myself, by the treatment of this agreeable subject, from the painful and troublesome impressions and recollections of my life at Weimar. He therefore very happily calls Tasso an elevated Werther.

"Then, concerning Faust, his remarks are no less clever, since he not only notes, as part of myself, the gloomy, discontented striving of the principal character, but also the scorn and the bitter irony of Mephistopheles."

In this, and a similar spirit of acknowledgment, Goethe often spoke of M. Ampere. We took a decided interest in him; we endeavored to picture to ourselves his personal appearance, and, if we could not succeed in this, we at least agreed that he must be a man of middle age to understand the reciprocal action of life and poetry on each other. We were, therefore, extremely surprised when M. Ampere arrived in Weimar a few days ago, and proved to be a lively youth, some twenty years old; and we were no less surprised when, in the course of further intercourse, he told us that the whole of the contributors of the. *Globe*, whose wisdom, moderation, and high degree of cultivation we had often admired, were only young people like himself.

"I can well comprehend," said I, "that a person may be young and may still produce something of importance—like Mérimée, for instance, who wrote excellent pieces in his twentieth year; but that any one at so early an age should have at his command such a comprehensive view, and such deep insight, as to attain such mature judgment as the gentlemen of the *Globe*, is to me something entirely new."

"To you, in your Heath,"[13] returned Goethe, "it has not been so easy; and we others also, in Central Germany, have been forced to buy our little wisdom dearly enough. Then we all lead a very isolated miserable sort of life! From the people,

[13] This doubtless refers to the Heath country in which Eckermann was born.—Trans.

properly so called, we derive very little culture. Our talents and men of brains are scattered over the whole of Germany. One is in Vienna, another in Berlin, another in Königsberg, another in Bonn or Düseldorf—all about a hundred miles apart from one another, so that personal contact and personal exchange of thought may be considered as rarities. I feel what this must be, when such men as Alexander von Humboldt come here, and in one single day lead me nearer to what I am seeking and what I require to know than I should have done for years in my own solitary way."

"But now conceive a city like Paris, where the highest talents of a great kingdom are all assembled in a single spot, and by daily intercourse, strife, and emulation, mutually instruct and advance each other; where the best works, both of nature and art, from all the kingdoms of the earth, are open to daily inspection; conceive this metropolis of the world, I say, where every walk over a bridge or across a square recalls some mighty past, and where some historical event is connected with every corner of a street. In addition to all this, conceive not the Paris of a dull, spiritless time, but the Paris of the nineteenth century, in which, during three generations, such men as Molière, Voltaire, Diderot, and the like, have kept up such a current of intellect as cannot be found twice in a single spot in the whole world, and you will comprehend that a man of talent like Ampere, who has grown up amid such abundance, can easily be something in his four-and-twentieth year.

"You said just now," said Goethe, "that you could well understand how any one in his twentieth year could write pieces as good as those of Mérimée. I have nothing to oppose to this; and I am, on the whole, quite of your opinion that good productiveness is easier than good judgment in a youthful man. But, in Germany, one had better not, when so young as Mérimée, attempt to produce anything so mature as he has done in his pieces of *Clara Gazul*. It is true, Schiller was very young when he wrote his *Robbers*, his *Love and Intrigue*, his *Fiesco*; but, to speak the truth, all three pieces are rather the utterances of an extraordinary talent than signs of mature cultivation in the author. This, however, is not Schiller's fault, but rather the result of the state of culture of his nation, and the great difficulty which we all experience in assisting ourselves on our solitary way.

"On the other hand, take up Béranger. He is the son of poor parents, the descendant of a poor tailor; at one time a poor printer's apprentice, then placed in some office with a small salary; he has never been to a classical school or university; and yet his songs are so full of mature cultivation, so full of wit and the most refined irony, and there is such artistic perfection and masterly handling of the language that he is the admiration, not only of France, but of all civilized Europe.

"But imagine this same Béranger—instead of being born in Paris, and brought up in this metropolis of the world—the son of a poor tailor in Jena or Weimar, and let him commence his career, in an equally miserable manner, in such small places—then ask yourself what fruit would have been produced by this same tree grown in such a soil and in such an atmosphere.

"Therefore, my good friend, I repeat that, if a talent is to be speedily and happily developed, the great point is that a great deal of intellect and sound culture should be current in a nation.

"We admire the tragedies of the ancient Greeks; but, to take a correct view of the case, we ought rather to admire the period and the nation in which their production was possible than the individual authors; for though each of these pieces differs a little from every other, and though one of these poets appears somewhat greater and more finished than the other, still, taking all things together, only one decided character runs through the whole.

"This is the character of grandeur, fitness, soundness, human perfection, elevated wisdom, sublime thought, pure, strong intuition, and whatever other qualities one might enumerate. But when we find all these qualities, not only in the dramatic works that have come down to us but also in lyrical and epic works, in the philosophers, the orators, and the historians, and in an equally high degree in the works of plastic art that have come down to us, we must feel convinced that such qualities did not merely belong to individuals, but were the current property of the nation and the whole period.

"Now, take up Burns. How is he great, except through the circumstance that the whole songs of his predecessors lived in the mouth of the people—that they were, so to speak, sung at his cradle; that, as a boy, he grew up amongst them, and the high excellence of these models so pervaded him that he had therein a living basis on which he could proceed further? Again, why is he great, but from this, that his own songs at once found susceptible ears amongst his compatriots; that, sung by reapers and sheaf-binders, they at once greeted him in the field; and that his boon-companions sang them to welcome him at the ale-house? Something was certainly to be done in this way.

"On the other hand, what a pitiful figure is made by us Germans! Of our old songs—no less important than those of Scotland—how many lived among the people in the days of my youth? Herder and his successors first began to collect them and rescue them from oblivion; then they were at least printed in the libraries. Then, more lately, what songs have not Bürger and Voss composed! Who can say that they are more insignificant or less popular than those of the excellent Burns? but which of them so lives among us that it greets us from the mouth of the people? They are written and printed, and they remain in the libraries, quite in accordance with the general fate of German poets. Of my own songs, how many live? Perhaps one or another of them may be sung by a pretty girl to the piano; but among the people, properly so called, they have no sound. With what sensations must I remember the time when passages from Tasso were sung to me by Italian fishermen!

"We Germans are of yesterday. We have indeed been properly cultivated for a century; but a few centuries more must still elapse before so much mind and elevated culture will become universal amongst our people that they will appreciate beauty like the Greeks, that they will be inspired by a beautiful song, and that it will be said of them 'it is long since they were barbarians.'"

Tuesday, December 16.—I dined today with Goethe alone, in his work-room. We talked on various literary topics.

"The Germans," said he, "cannot cease to be Philistines. They are now squabbling about some verses, which are printed both in Schiller's works and mine, and fancy it is important to ascertain which really belong to Schiller and which to me; as if anything could be gained by such investigation—as if the existence of such things were not enough. Friends, such as Schiller and I, intimate for years, with the same interests, in habits of daily intercourse, and under reciprocal obligations, live so completely in each other that it is hardly possible to decide to which of the two the particular thoughts belong.

"We have made many distiches together; sometimes I gave the thought, and Schiller made the verse; sometimes the contrary was the case; sometimes he made one line, and I the other. What matters the mine and thine? One must be a thorough Philistine, indeed, to attach the slightest importance to the solution of such questions."

"Something similar," said I, "often happens in the literary world, when people, for instance, doubt the originality of this or that celebrated man, and seek to trace out the sources from whence he obtained his cultivation."

"That is very ridiculous," said Goethe; "we might as well question a strong man about the oxen, sheep, and swine, which he has eaten, and which have given him strength.

"We are indeed born with faculties; but we owe our development to a thousand influences of the great world, from which we appropriate to ourselves what we can, and what is suitable to us. I owe much to the Greeks and French; I am infinitely indebted to Shakespeare, Sterne, and Goldsmith; but in saying this I do not show the sources of my culture; that would be an endless as well as an unnecessary task. What is important is to have a soul which loves truth, and receives it wherever it finds it.

"Besides, the world is now so old, so many eminent men have lived and thought for thousands of years, that there is little new to be discovered or expressed. Even my theory of colors is not entirely new. Plato, Leonardo da Vinci, any many other excellent men, have before me found and expressed the same thing in a detached form: my merit is, that I have found it also, that I have said it again, and that I have striven to bring the truth once more into a confused world.

"The truth must be repeated over and over again, because error is repeatedly preached among us, not only by individuals, but by the masses. In periodicals and cyclopædias, in schools and universities; everywhere, in fact, error prevails, and is quite easy in the feeling that it has a decided majority on its side.

"Often, too, people teach truth and error together, and stick to the latter. Thus, a short time ago, I read in an English cyclopædia the doctrine of the origin of Blue. First came the correct view of Leonardo da Vinci, but then followed, as quietly as possible, the error of Newton, coupled with remarks that this was to be adhered to because it was the view generally adopted."

I could not help laughing with surprise when I heard this. "Every wax-taper," I said, "every illuminated cloud of smoke from the kitchen, that has anything dark behind it, every morning mist, when it lies before a steady spot, daily convinces me of the origin of blue color, and makes me comprehend the blueness of the sky. What the Newtonians mean when they say that the air has the property of absorbing other colors, and of repelling blue alone, I cannot at all understand, nor do I see what use or pleasure is to be derived from a doctrine in which all thought stands still, and all sound observation completely vanishes."

"My good innocent friend," said Goethe, "these people do not care a jot about thoughts and observations. They are satisfied if they have only words which they can pass as current, as was well shown and not ill-expressed by my own Mephistopheles:

> "Mind, above all, you stick to words,
> Thus through the safe gate you will go
> Into the fane of certainty;
> For when ideas begin to fail
> A word will aptly serve your turn," etc.

Goethe recited this passage laughing, and seemed altogether in the best humor. "It is a good thing," said he, "that all is already in print, and I shall go on printing as long as I have anything to say against false doctrine, and those who disseminate it.

"We have now excellent men rising up in natural science," he continued, after a pause, "and I am glad to see them. Others begin well, but afterwards fall off; their predominating subjectivity leads them astray. Others, again, set too much value on facts, and collect an infinite number, by which nothing is proved. On the whole, there is a want of originating mind to penetrate back to the original phenomena, and master the particulars that make their appearance."

A short visit interrupted our discourse, but when we were again alone the conversation returned to poetry, and I told Goethe that I had of late been once more studying his little poems, and had dwelt especially upon two of them, viz., the ballad[14] about the children and the old man, and the "Happy Couple" (*die glücklichen Gatten*).

"I myself set some value on these two poems," said Goethe, "although the German public have hitherto not been able to make much out of them."

"In the ballad," I said, "a very copious subject is brought into a very limited compass, by means of all sorts of poetical forms and artifices, among which I especially praise the expedient of making the old man tell the children's past history down to the point where the present moment comes in, and the rest is developed before our eyes."

"I carried the ballad a long time about in my head," said Goethe, "before I wrote it down. Whole years of reflection are comprised in it, and I made three or four trials before I could reduce it to its present shape."

"The poem of the 'Happy Couple,'" continued Goethe, "is likewise rich in

---

[14] This poem is simply entitled "Ballade," and begins "Herein, O du Guter! du Alter herein!" — *Trans.*

motives; whole landscapes and passages of human life appear in it, warmed by the sunlight of a charming spring sky, which is diffused over the whole."

"I have always liked that poem," said Goethe, "and I am glad that you have regarded it with particular interest. The ending of the whole pleasantry with a double christening is, I think, pretty enough."

We then came to the *Bürgergeneral* (Citizengeneral); with respect to which I said that I had been lately reading this piece with an Englishman, and that we had both felt the strongest desire to see it represented on the stage. "As far as the spirit of the work is concerned," said I, "there is nothing antiquated about it; and with respect to the details of dramatic development, there is not a touch that does not seem designed for the stage."

"It was a very good piece in its time," said Goethe, "and caused us many a pleasant evening. It was, indeed, excellently cast, and had been so admirably studied that the dialogue moved along as glibly as possible. Malcolmi played Märten, and nothing could be more perfect.

"The part of Schnaps," said I, "seems to me no less felicitous. Indeed, I should not think there were many better or more thankful parts in the repertoire. There is in this personage, as in the whole piece, a clearness, an actual presence, to the utmost extent that can be desired for a theatre. The scene where he comes in with the knapsack, and produces the things one after another, where he puts the *moustache* on Märten, and decks himself with the cap of liberty, uniform, and sword, is among the best." "This scene," said Goethe, "used always to be very successful on our stage. Then the knapsack, with the articles in it, had really an historical existence. I found it in the time of the Revolution, on my travels along the French border, when the emigrants, on their flight, had passed through, and one of them might have lost it or thrown it away. The articles it contained were just the same as in the piece. I wrote the scene upon it, and the knapsack, with all its appurtenances, was always introduced, to the no small delight of our actors."

The question whether the *Bürgergeneral* could still be played with any interest or profit, was for a while the subject of our conversation.

Goethe then asked about my progress in French literature, and I told him that I still took up Voltaire from time to time, and that the great talent of this man gave me the purest delight.

"I still know but little of him," said I; "I keep to his short poems addressed to persons, which I read over and over again, and which I cannot lay aside."

"Indeed," said Goethe, "all is good which is written by so great a genius as Voltaire, though I cannot excuse all his profanity. But you are right to give so much time to those little poems addressed to persons; they are unquestionably among the most charming of his works. There is not a line which is not full of thought, clear, bright, and graceful."

"And we see," said I, "his relations to all the great and mighty of the world, and remark with pleasure the distinguished position taken by himself, inasmuch as he seems to feel himself equal to the highest, and we never find that any majesty can embarrass his free mind even for a moment."

"Yes," said Goethe, "he bore himself like a man of rank. And with all his freedom and audacity, he ever kept within the limits of strict propriety, which is, perhaps, saying still more. I may cite the Empress of Austria as an authority in such matters; she has repeatedly assured me, that in those poems of Voltaire's, there is no trace of crossing the line of *convenance*."

"Does your excellency," said I, "remember the short poem in which he makes to the Princess of Prussia, afterwards Queen of Sweden, a pretty declaration of love, by saying that he dreamed of being elevated to the royal dignity?"

"It is one of his best," said Goethe, and he recited the lines—

> "Je vous aimais, princesse, et j'osais vous le dire;
> Les Dieux et mon reveil ne m'ont pas tout ôté,
> Je n'ai perdu que mon empire."

"How pretty that is! And never did poet have his talent so completely at command every moment as Voltaire. I remember an anecdote, when he had been for some time on a visit to Madame du Chatelet. Just as he was going away, and the carriage was standing at the door, he received a letter from a great number of young girls in a neighboring convent, who wished to play the 'Death of Julius Cæsar' on the birthday of their abbess, and begged him to write them a prologue. The case was too delicate for a refusal; so Voltaire at once called for pen and paper, and wrote the desired prologue, standing, upon the mantlepiece. It is a poem of perhaps twenty lines, thoroughly digested, finished, perfectly suited to the occasion, and, in short, of the very best class."

"I am very desirous to read it," said I.

"I doubt," said Goethe, "whether you will find it in your collection. It has only lately come to light, and, indeed, he wrote hundreds of such poems, of which many may still be scattered about among private persons."

"I found of late a passage in Lord Byron," said I, "from which I perceived with delight that even Byron had an extraordinary esteem for Voltaire. We may see in his works how much he liked to read, study, and make use of Voltaire."

"Byron," said Goethe, "knew too well where anything was to be got, and was too clever not to draw from this universal source of light."

The conversation then turned entirely upon Byron and several of his works, and Goethe found occasion to repeat many of his former expressions of admiration for that great genius.

"To all that your excellency says of Byron," said I, "I agree from the bottom of my heart; but, however great and remarkable that poet may be as a genius, I very much doubt whether a decided gain for pure human culture is to be derived from his writings."

"There I must contradict you," said Goethe; "the audacity and grandeur of Byron must certainly tend towards culture. We should take care not to be always looking for it in the decidedly pure and moral. Everything that is great promotes cultivation as soon as we are aware of it."

* * * * *

Thursday, February 12.—Goethe read me the thoroughly noble poem, "Kein Wesen kann zu nichts zerfallen" (No being can dissolve to nothing), which he had lately written.

"I wrote this poem," said he, "in contradiction to my lines—

'Denn alles muss zu nichts zerfallen
Wenn es im Seyn beharren will,' etc.

('For all must melt away to nothing
Would it continue still to be')—

which are stupid, and which my Berlin friends, on the occasion of the late assembly of natural philosophers, set up in golden letters, to my annoyance."

The conversation turned on the great mathematician, Lagrange, whose excellent character Goethe highly extolled.

"He was a good man," said he, "and on that very account, a great man. For when a good man is gifted with talent, he always works morally for the salvation of the world, as poet, philosopher, artist, or in whatever way it may be.

"I am glad," continued Goethe, "that you had an opportunity yesterday of knowing Coudray better. He says little in general society, but, here among ourselves, you have seen what an excellent mind and character reside in the man. He had, at first, much opposition to encounter, but he has now fought through it all and enjoys the entire confidence and favor of the court. Coudray is one of the most skilful architects of our time. He has adhered to me and I to him, and this has been of service to us both. If I had but known him fifty years ago!"

We then talked about Goethe's own architectural knowledge. I remarked that he must have acquired much in Italy.

"Italy gave me an idea of earnestness and greatness," said he, "but no practical skill. The building of the castle here in Weimar advanced me more than anything. I was obliged to assist, and even to make drawings of entablatures. I had a certain advantage over the professional people, because I was superior to them in intention."

We talked of Zelter.

"I have a letter from him," said Goethe, "in which he complains that the performance of the oratorio of the Messiah was spoiled for him by one of his female scholars, who sang an aria too weakly and sentimentally. Weakness is a characteristic of our age. My hypothesis is, that it is a consequence of the efforts made in Germany to get rid of the French. Painters, natural philosophers, sculptors, musicians, poets, with but few exceptions, all are weak, and the general mass is no better."

"Yet I do not give up the hope," said I, "of seeing suitable music composed for *Faust*."

"Quite impossible!" said Goethe. "The awful and repulsive passages which must occasionally occur, are not in the style of the time. The music should be like that of Don Juan. Mozart should have composed for *Faust*. Meyerbeer would, perhaps, be capable; but he would not touch anything of the kind;[15] he is too much engaged with the Italian theatres."

Afterwards—I do not recollect in connection to what—Goethe made the following important remark:

"All that is great and skilful exists with the minority. There have been ministers who have had both king and people against them, and have carried out their great plans alone. It is not to be imagined that reason can ever be popular. Passions and feelings may become popular; but reason always remains the sole property of a few eminent individuals."

Sunday, December 6.—Today, after dinner, Goethe read me the first scene of the second act of *Faust*.[16] The effect was great, and gave me a high satisfaction. We are once more transported into Faust's study, where Mephistopheles finds all just as he had left it. He takes from the hook Faust's old study-gown, and a thousand moths and insects flutter out from it. By the directions of Mephistopheles as to where these are to settle down, the locality is brought very clearly before our eyes. He puts on the gown, while Faust lies behind a curtain in a state of paralysis, intending to play the doctor's part once more. He pulls the bell, which gives such an awful tone among the old solitary convent halls, that the doors spring open and the walls tremble. The servant rushes in, and finds in Faust's seat Mephistopheles, whom he does not recognize, but for whom he has respect. In answer to inquiries he gives news of Wagner, who has now become a celebrated man, and is hoping for the return of his master. He is, we hear, at this moment deeply occupied in his laboratory, seeking to produce a Homunculus. The servant retires, and the bachelor enters—the same whom we knew some years before as a shy young student, when Mephistopheles (in Faust's gown) made game of him. He is now become a man, and is so full of conceit that even Mephistopheles can do nothing with him, but moves his chair further and further, and at last addresses the pit.

Goethe read the scene quite to the end. I was pleased with his youthful productive strength, and with the closeness of the whole. "As the conception," said Goethe, "is so old—for I have had it in my mind for fifty years—the materials have accumulated to such a degree, that the difficult operation is to separate and reject. The invention of the whole second part is really as old as I say; but it may be an advantage that I have not written it down till now, when my knowledge of the world is so much clearer. I am like one who in his youth has a great deal of small silver and copper money, which in the course of his life he constantly changes for the better, so that at last the property of his youth stands before him in pieces of pure gold."

------

[15] A It must be borne in mind that this was said before the appearance of "Robert le Diable," which was first produced in Paris, in November, 1831.—*Trans.*

[16] B That is, the second act of the second part of "Faust," which was not published entire till after Goethe's death.—*Trans.*

We spoke about the character of the Bachelor. "Is he not meant," said I, "to represent a certain class of ideal philosophers?"

"No," said Goethe, "the arrogance which is peculiar to youth, and of which we had such striking examples after our war for freedom, is personified in him. Indeed, every one believes in his youth that the world really began with him, and that all merely exists for his sake.

"Thus, in the East, there was actually a man who every morning collected his people about him, and would not go to work till he had commanded the sun to rise. But he was wise enough not to speak his command till the sun of its own accord was really on the point of appearing."

Goethe remained a while absorbed in silent thought; then he began as follows: "When one is old one thinks of worldly matters otherwise than when one is young. Thus I cannot but think that the demons, to teaze and make sport with men, have placed among them single figures, which are so alluring that every one strives after them, and so great that nobody reaches them. Thus they set up Raffael, with whom thought and act were equally perfect; some distinguished followers have approached him, but none have equalled him. Thus, too, they set up Mozart as something unattainable in music; and thus Shakespeare in poetry. I know what you can say against this thought; but I only mean natural character, the great innate qualities. Thus, too, Napoleon is unattainable. That the Russians were so moderate as not to go to Constantinople is indeed very great; but we find a similar trait in Napoleon, for he had the moderation not to go to Rome."

Much was associated with this copious theme; I thought to myself in silence that the demons had intended something of the kind with Goethe, inasmuch as he is a form too alluring not to be striven after, and too great to be reached.

Wednesday, December 16.—Today, after dinner, Goethe read me the second scene of the second act of "Faust," where Mephistopheles visits Wagner, who is on the point of making a human being by chemical means. The work succeeds; the Homunculus appears in the phial, as a shining being, and is at once active. He repels Wagner's questions upon incomprehensible subjects; reasoning is not his business; he wishes to act, and begins with our hero, Faust, who, in his paralyzed condition, needs a higher aid. As a being to whom the present is perfectly clear and transparent, the Homunculus sees into the soul of the sleeping Faust, who, enraptured by a lovely dream, beholds Leda visited by swans, while she is bathing in a pleasant spot. The Homunculus, by describing this dream, brings a most charming picture before our eyes. Mephistopheles sees nothing of it, and the Homunculus taunts him with his northern nature.

"Generally," said Goethe, "you will perceive that Mephistopheles appears to disadvantage beside the Homunculus, who is like him in clearness of intellect, and so much superior to him in his tendency to the beautiful and to a useful activity. He styles him cousin; for such spiritual beings as this Homunculus, not yet saddened and limited by a thorough assumption of humanity, were classed with the demons, and thus there is a sort of relationship between the two."

"Certainly," said I, "Mephistopheles appears here in a subordinate situation;

yet I cannot help thinking that he has had a secret influence on the production of the Homunculus. We have known him in this way before; and, indeed, in the 'Helena' he always appears as a being secretly working. Thus he again elevates himself with regard to the whole, and in his lofty repose he can well afford to put up with a little in particulars."

"Your feeling of the position is very correct," said Goethe; "indeed, I have doubted whether I ought not to put some verses into the mouth of Mephistopheles as he goes to Wagner, and the Homunculus is still in a state of formation, so that his cooperation may be expressed and rendered plain to the reader.

"It would do no harm," said I. "Yet this is intimated by the words with which Mephistopheles closes the scene—

> Am Ende hangen wir doch ab
> Von Creaturen die wir machten.
> We are dependent after all,
> On creatures that we make."

"True," said Goethe, "that would be almost enough for the attentive; but I will think about some additional verses."

"But," said I, "those concluding words are very great, and will not easily be penetrated to their full extent."

"I think," said Goethe, "I have given them a bone to pick. A father who has six sons is a lost man, let him do what he may. Kings and ministers, too, who have raised many persons to high places, may have something to think about from their own experience."

Faust's dream about Leda again came into my head, and I regarded this as a most important feature in the composition.

"It is wonderful to me," said I, "how the several parts of such a work bear upon, perfect, and sustain one another! By this dream of Leda, *Helena* gains its proper foundation. There we have a constant allusion to swans and the child of a swan; but here we have the act itself, and when we come afterwards to Helena, with the sensible impression of such a situation, how much more clear and perfect does all appear!"

Goethe said I was right, and was pleased that I remarked this.

"Thus you will see," said he, "that in these earlier acts the chords of the classic and romantic are constantly struck, so that, as on a rising ground, where both forms of poetry are brought out, and in some sort balance each other, we may ascend to 'Helena.'

"The French," continued Goethe, "now begin to think justly of these matters. Both classic and romantic, say they, are equally good. The only point is to use these forms with judgment, and to be capable of excellence. You can be absurd in both, and then one is as worthless as the other. This, I think, is rational enough, and may content us for a while."

* * * * *

1830.

Sunday, March 14. — This evening at Goethe's. He showed me all the treasures, now put in order, from the chest which he had received from David, and with the unpacking of which I had found him occupied some days ago. The plaster medallions, with the profiles of the principal young poets of France, he had laid in order side by side upon tables. On this occasion, he spoke once more of the extraordinary talent of David, which was as great in conception as in execution. He also showed me a number of the newest works, which had been presented to him, through the medium of David, as gifts from the most distinguished men of the romantic school. I saw works by St. Veuve, Ballanche, Victor Hugo, Balzac, Alfred de Vigny, Jules Janin, and others.

"David," said he, "has prepared happy days for me by this present. The young poets have already occupied me the whole week, and afford me new life by the fresh impressions which I receive from them. I shall make a separate catalogue of these much esteemed portraits and books, and shall give them both a special place in my collection of works of art and my library."

One could see from Goethe's manner that this homage from the young poets of France afforded him the heartiest delight.

He then read something from the *Studies*, by Emile Deschamps. He praised the translation of the *Bride of Corinth*, as faithful, and very successful.

"I possess," said he, "the manuscript of an Italian translation of this poem, which gives the original, even to the rhymes."

The Bride of Corinth induced Goethe to speak of the rest of his ballads. "I owe them, in a great measure, to Schiller," said he, "who impelled me to them, because he always wanted something new for his *Horen*. I had already carried them in my head for many years; they occupied my mind as pleasant images, as beautiful dreams, which came and went, and by playing with which my fancy made me happy. I unwillingly resolved to bid farewell to these brilliant visions, which had so long been my solace, by embodying them in poor, inadequate words. When I saw them on paper, I regarded them with a mixture of sadness. I felt as if I were about to be separated for ever from a beloved friend."

"At other times," continued Goethe, "it has been totally different with my poems. They have been preceded by no impressions or forebodings, but have come suddenly upon me, and have insisted on being composed immediately, so that I have felt an instinctive and dreamy impulse to write them down on the spot. In such a somnambulistic condition, it has often happened that I have had a sheet of paper lying before me all on one side, and I have not discovered it till all has been written, or I have found no room to write any more. I have possessed many such sheets written crossways, but they have been lost one after another, and I regret that I can no longer show any proofs of such poetic abstraction."

The conversation then returned to the French literature, and the modern ultra-romantic tendency of some not unimportant men of genius. Goethe was of opinion that this poetic revolution, which was still in its infancy, would be very favorable to literature, but very prejudicial to the individual authors who effect it.

"Extremes are never to be avoided in any revolution," said he. "In a political one, nothing is generally desired in the beginning but the abolition of abuses; but before people are aware, they are deep in bloodshed and horror. Thus the French, in their present literary revolution, desired nothing at first but a freer form; however, they will not stop there, but will reject the traditional contents together with the form. They begin to declare the representation of noble sentiments and deeds as tedious, and attempt to treat of all sorts of abominations. Instead of the beautiful subjects from Grecian mythology, there are devils, witches, and vampires, and the lofty heroes of antiquity must give place to jugglers and galley slaves. This is piquant! This is effective! But after the public has once tasted this highly seasoned food, and has become accustomed to it, it will always long for more, and that stronger. A young man of talent, who would produce an effect and be acknowledged, and who is great enough to go his own way, must accommodate himself to the taste of the day—nay, must seek to outdo his predecessors in the horrible and frightful. But in this chase after outward means of effect, all profound study, and all gradual and thorough development of the talent and the man from within, is entirely neglected. And this is the greatest injury which can befall a talent, although literature in general will gain by this tendency of the moment."

"But," added I, "how can an attempt which destroys individual talents be favorable to literature in general?"

"The extremes and excrescences which I have described," returned Goethe, "will gradually disappear; but at last this great advantage will remain—besides a freer form, richer and more diversified subjects will have been attained, and no object of the broadest world and the most manifold life will be any longer excluded as unpoetical. I compare the present literary epoch to a state of violent fever, which is not in itself good and desirable, but of which improved health is the happy consequence. That abomination which now often constitutes the whole subject of a poetical work, will in future only appear as an useful expedient; aye, the pure and the noble, which is now abandoned for the moment, will soon be resought with additional ardor."

"It is surprising to me," remarked I, "that even Mérimée, who is one of your favorites, has entered upon this ultra-romantic path, through the horrible subjects of his *Guzla*."

"Mérimée," returned Goethe, "has treated these things very differently from his fellow-authors. These poems certainly are not deficient in various horrible *motives*, such as churchyards, nightly crossways, ghosts and vampires; but the repulsive themes do not touch the intrinsic merit of the poet. On the contrary, he treats them from a certain objective distance, and, as it were, with irony. He goes to work with them like an artist, to whom it is an amusement to try anything of the sort. He has, as I have said before, quite renounced himself, nay, he has ever renounced the Frenchman, and that to such a degree that at first these poems of Guzla were deemed real Illyrian popular poems, and thus little was wanting for the success of the imposition he had intended."

"Mérimée," continued Goethe, "is indeed a thorough fellow! Indeed, generally, more power and genius are required for the objective treatment of a subject than is supposed. Thus, too, Lord Byron, notwithstanding his predominant personality, has sometimes had the power of renouncing himself altogether, as may be seen in some of his dramatic pieces, particularly in his *Marino Faliero*. In this piece one quite forgets that Lord Byron, or even an Englishman, wrote it. We live entirely in Venice, and entirely in the time in which the action takes place. The personages speak quite from themselves and from their own condition, without having any of the subjective feelings, thoughts, and opinions of the poet. That is as it should be. Of our young French romantic writers of the exaggerating sort, one cannot say as much. What I have read of them—poems, novels, dramatic works—have all borne the personal coloring of the author, and none of them ever makes me forget that a Parisian—that a Frenchman—wrote them. Even in the treatment of foreign subjects one still remains in France and Paris, quite absorbed in all the wishes, necessities, conflicts, and fermentations of the present day."

"Béranger also," I threw in experimentally, "has only expressed the situation of the great metropolis, and his own interior."

"That is a man," said Goethe, "whose power of representation and whose interior are worth something. In him is all the substance of an important personality. Béranger is a nature most happily endowed, firmly grounded in himself, purely developed from himself, and quite in harmony with himself. He has never asked—what would suit the times? what produces an effect? what pleases? what are others doing?—in order that he might do the like. He has always worked only from the core of his own nature, without troubling himself as to what the public, or what this or that party, expects. He has certainly, at different critical epochs, been influenced by the mood, wishes, and necessities of the people; but that has only confirmed him in himself, by proving to him that his own nature is in harmony with that of the people; and has never seduced him into expressing anything but what already lay in his heart.

"You know that I am, upon the whole, no friend to what is called political poems, but such as Béranger has composed I can tolerate. With him there is nothing snatched out of the air, nothing of merely imagined or imaginary interest; he never shoots at random; but, on the contrary, has always the most decided, the most important subjects. His affectionate admiration of Napoleon, and his reminiscences of the great warlike deeds which were performed under him, and that at a time when these recollections were a consolation to the somewhat oppressed French; then his hatred of the domination of priests, and of the darkness which threatened to return with the Jesuits—these are things to which one cannot refuse hearty sympathy. And how masterly is his treatment on all occasions! How he turns about and rounds off every subject in his own mind before he expresses it! And then, when all is matured, what wit, spirit, irony, and persiflage, and what heartiness, naivete, and grace, are unfolded at every step! His songs have every year made millions of joyous men; they always flow glibly from the tongue, even with the working-classes, whilst they are so far elevated above the level of the commonplace, that the populace, in converse with these pleasant spirits, becomes accustomed and compelled to think itself better and nobler. What more would you have? and, altogether, what higher praise could be given to a poet?"

"He is excellent, unquestionably!" returned I. "You know how I loved him for years, and can imagine how it gratifies me to hear you speak of him thus. But if I must say which of his songs I prefer, his amatory poems please me more than his political, in which the particular references and allusions are not always clear to me."

"That happens to be your case," returned Goethe; "the political poems were not written for you; but ask the French, and they will tell you what is good in them. Besides, a political poem, under the most fortunate circumstances, is to be looked upon only as the organ of a single nation, and, in most cases, only as the organ of a single party; but it is seized with enthusiasm by this nation and this party when it is good. Again, a political poem should always be looked upon as the mere result of a certain state of the times; which passes by, and with respect to succeeding times takes from the poem the value which it derived from the subject. As for Béranger, his was no hard task. Paris is France. All the important interests of his great country are concentrated in the capital, and there have their proper life and their proper echo. Besides, in most of his political songs he is by no means to be regarded as the mere organ of a single party; on the contrary, the things against which he writes are for the most part of so universal and national an interest, that the poet is almost always heard as a great *voice* of the people. With us, in Germany, such a thing is not possible. We have no city, nay, we have no country, of which we could decidedly say—*Here is Germany*! If we inquire in Vienna, the answer is—this is Austria! and if in Berlin, the answer is—this is Prussia! Only sixteen years ago, when we tried to get rid of the French, was Germany everywhere. Then a political poet could have had an universal effect; but there was no need of one! The universal necessity, and the universal feeling of disgrace, had seized upon the nation like something dæmonic; the inspiring fire which the poet might have kindled was already burning everywhere of its own accord. Still, I will not deny that Arndt, Körner, and Rückert, have had some effect."

"You have been reproached," remarked I, rather inconsiderately, "for not taking up arms at that great period, or at least cooperating as a poet."

"Let us leave that point alone, my good friend," returned Goethe. "It is an absurd world, which does not know what it wants, and which one must allow to have its own way. How could I take up arms without hatred, and how could I hate without youth? If such an emergency had befallen me when twenty years old, I should certainly not have been the last; but it found me as one who had already passed the first sixties.

"Besides, we cannot all serve our country in the same way, but each does his best, according as God has endowed him. I have toiled hard enough during half a century. I can say, that in those things which nature has appointed for my daily work, I have permitted myself no repose or relaxation night or day, but have always striven, investigated, and done as much, and that as well, as I could. If every one can say the same of himself, it will prove well with all."

"The fact is," said I, by way of conciliation, "that you should not be vexed at that reproach, but should rather feel flattered at it. For what does it show but that the opinion of the world concerning you is so great that it desires that he who has done more for the culture of his nation than any other should at last do everything!"

"I will not say what I think," returned Goethe. "There is more ill-will towards me hidden beneath that remark than you are aware of. I feel therein a new form of the old hatred with which people have persecuted me, and endeavored quietly to wound me for years. I know very well that I am an eyesore to many; that they would all willingly get rid of me; and that, since they cannot touch my talent, they aim at my character. Now, it is said, I am proud; now, egotistical; now, full of envy towards young men of genius; now, immersed in sensuality; now, without Christianity; and now, without love for my native country, and my own dear Germans. You have now known me sufficiently for years, and you feel what all that talk is worth. But if you would learn what I have suffered, read my '*Xenien*', and it will be clear to you, from my retorts, how people have from time to time sought to embitter my life.

"A German author is a German martyr! Yes, my friend, you will not find it otherwise! And I myself can scarcely complain; none of the others has fared better—most have fared worse; and in England and France it is quite the same as with us. What did not Molière suffer? What Rousseau and Voltaire? Byron was driven from England by evil tongues, and would have fled to the end of the world, if an early death had not delivered him from the Philistines and their hatred.

"And if it were only the narrow-minded masses that persecuted noble men! But no! one gifted man and one genius persecutes another; Platen scandalizes Heine, and Heine Platen, and each seeks to make the other hateful; while the world is wide enough for all to live and to let live; and every one has an enemy in his own talent, who gives him quite enough to do.

"To write military songs, and sit in a room! That forsooth was my duty! To have written them in the bivouac, when the horses at the enemy's outposts are heard neighing at night, would have been well enough; however, that was not my life and not my business, but that of Theodore Körner. His war-songs suit him perfectly. But to me, who am not of a warlike nature, and who have no warlike sense, war-songs would have been a mask which would have fitted my face very badly.

"I have never affected anything in my poetry. I have never uttered anything which I have not experienced, and which has not urged me to production. I have composed love-songs only when I have loved. How could I write songs of hatred without hating! And, between ourselves, I did not hate the French, although I thanked God that we were free from them. How could I, to whom culture and barbarism are alone of importance, hate a nation which is among the most cultivated of the earth, and to which I owe so great a part of my own cultivation?

"Altogether," continued Goethe, "national hatred is something peculiar. You will always find it strongest and most violent where there is the lowest degree of culture. But there is a degree where it vanishes altogether, and where one stands to a certain extent above nations, and feels the weal or woe of a neighboring people, as if it had happened to one's own. This degree of culture was conformable to my nature, and I had become strengthened in it long before I had reached my sixtieth year."

* * * * *

1832.

Sunday, March 11.—The conversation turned upon the great men who had lived before Christ, among the Chinese, the Indians, the Persians, and the Greeks; and it was remarked, that the divine power had been as operative in them as in some of the great Jews of the Old Testament. We then came to the question how far God influenced the great natures of the present world in which we live?

"To hear people speak," said Goethe, "one would almost believe that they were of opinion that God had withdrawn into silence since those old times, and that man was now placed quite upon his own feet, and had to see how he could get on without God, and his daily invisible breath. In religious and moral matters a divine influence is indeed still allowed, but in matters of science and art it is believed that they are merely earthly and nothing but the product of human powers.

SCHILLER'S GARDEN HOUSE AT JENA (DRAWING BY GOETHE)

"Let any one only try, with human will and human power, to produce something which may be compared with the creations that bear the names of Mozart, Raphael, or Shakespeare. I know very well that these three noble beings are not the only ones, and that in every province of art innumerable excellent geniuses have operated, who have produced things as perfectly good as those just mentioned. But if they were as great as those, they rose above ordinary human nature, and in the same proportion were as divinely endowed as they.

"And, after all, what does it all come to? God did not retire to rest after the well-known six days of creation, but, on the contrary, is constantly active as on the first. It would have been for Him a poor occupation to compose this heavy world out of simple elements, and to keep it rolling in the sunbeams from year to year, if He had not had the plan of founding a nursery for a world of spirits upon this material basis. So He is now constantly active in higher natures to attract the lower ones."

Goethe was silent. But I cherished his great and good words in my heart.

Early in March.[17]—Goethe mentioned at table that he had received a visit from Baron Carl Von Spiegel, and that he had been pleased with him beyond measure.

"He is a very fine young man," said Goethe; "in his mien and manners he has something by which the nobleman is seen at once. He could as little dissemble his descent as any one could deny a higher intellect; for birth and intellect both give him who once possesses them a stamp which no incognito can conceal. Like beauty, these are powers which one cannot approach without feeling that they are of a higher nature."

Some days later.—We talked of the tragic idea of Destiny among the Greeks.

"It no longer suits our way of thinking," said Goethe; "it is obsolete, and is also in contradiction with our religious views. If a modern poet introduces such antique ideas into a drama, it always has an air of affectation. It is a costume which is long since out of fashion, and which, like the Roman toga, no longer suits us.

"It is better for us moderns to say with Napoleon, 'Politics are Destiny.' But let us beware of saying, with our latest literati, that politics are poetry, or a suitable subject for the poet. The English poet Thomson wrote a very good poem on the Seasons, but a very bad one on Liberty, and that not from want of poetry in the poet, but from want of poetry in the subject."

"If a poet would work politically, he must give himself up to a party; and so soon as he does that, he is lost as a poet; he must bid farewell to his free spirit, his unbiased view, and draw over his ears the cap of bigotry and blind hatred.

"The poet, as a man and citizen, will love his native land; but the native land of his poetic powers and poetic action is the good, noble, and beautiful, which is confined to no particular province or country, and which he seizes upon and forms wherever he finds it. Therein is he like the eagle, who hovers with free gaze over whole countries, and to whom it is of no consequence whether the hare on which he pounces is running in Prussia or in Saxony.

"And, then, what is meant by love of one's country? What is meant by patriotic deeds? If the poet has employed a life in battling with pernicious prejudices, in setting aside narrow views, in enlightening the minds, purifying the tastes, ennobling the feelings and thoughts of his countrymen, what better could he have done? How could he have acted more patriotically?

"To make such ungrateful and unsuitable demands upon a poet is just as if <u>one required the</u> captain of a regiment to show himself a patriot, by taking part in

[17] In the original book this conversation follows immediately the one of December 21, 1831, and with the remainder of the book is prefaced thus:—"The following I noted down shortly afterwards (that is, after they took place) from memory."—Trans.

political innovations and thus neglecting his proper calling. The captain's country is his regiment, and he will show himself an excellent patriot by troubling himself about political matters only so far as they concern him, and bestowing all his mind and all his care on the battalions under him, trying so to train and discipline them that they may do their duty if ever their native land should be in peril.

THE MOAT AT JENA (DRAWING BY GOETHE)

"I hate all bungling like sin, but most of all bungling in state-affairs, which produces nothing but mischief to thousands and millions.

"You know that, on the whole, I care little what is written about me; but yet it comes to my ears, and I know well enough that, hard as I have toiled all my life, all my labors are as nothing in the eyes of certain people, just because I have disdained to mingle in political parties. To please such people I must have become a member of a Jacobin club, and preached bloodshed and murder. However, not a word more upon this wretched subject, lest I become unwise in railing against folly."

In the same manner he blamed the political course, so much praised by others, of Uhland.

"Mind," said he, "the politician will devour the poet. To be a member of the States, and to live amid daily jostlings and excitements, is not for the delicate nature of a poet. His song will cease, and that is in some sort to be lamented. Swabia has plenty of men, sufficiently well educated, well meaning, able, and eloquent, to be members of the States, but only one poet of Uhland's class."

* * * * *

The last stranger whom Goethe entertained as his guest was the eldest son of Frau von Arnim; the last words he wrote were some verses in the album of this young friend.

* * * * *

The morning after Goethe's death, a deep desire seized me to look once again upon his earthly garment. His faithful servant, Frederic, opened for me the chamber in which he was laid out. Stretched upon his back, he reposed as if asleep; profound peace and security reigned in the features of his sublimely noble countenance. The mighty brow seemed yet to harbor thoughts. I wished for a lock of his hair; but reverence prevented me from cutting it off. The body lay naked, wrapped only in a white sheet; large pieces of ice had been placed near it, to keep it fresh as long as possible. Frederic drew aside the sheet, and I was astonished at the divine magnificence of the limbs. The breast was powerful, broad, and arched; the arms and thighs were full, and softly muscular; the feet were elegant, and of the most perfect shape; nowhere, on the whole body, was there a trace either of fat or of leanness and decay. A perfect man lay in great beauty before me; and the rapture which the sight caused made me forget for a moment that the immortal spirit had left such an abode. I laid my hand on his heart—there was a deep silence—and I turned away to give free vent to my suppressed tears.

VIEW INTO THE SAALE VALLEY NEAR JENA (DRAWING BY GOETHE)

Lector House believes that a society develops through a two-fold approach of continuous learning and adaptation, which is derived from the study of classic literary works spread across the historic timeline of literature records. Therefore, we aim at reviving, repairing and redeveloping all those inaccessible or damaged but historically as well as culturally important literature across subjects so that the future generations may have an opportunity to study and learn from past works to embark upon a journey of creating a better future.

This book is a result of an effort made by Lector House towards making a contribution to the preservation and repair of original ancient works which might hold historical significance to the approach of continuous learning across subjects.

HAPPY READING & LEARNING!

LECTOR HOUSE LLP
E-MAIL: lectorpublishing@gmail.com

www.ingramcontent.com/pod-product-compliance
Lightning Source LLC
LaVergne TN
LVHW091148180726
843490LV00004B/1372